4/5

Gwen Troake's Country Cookbook

Gwen Troake's
Country Cookbook

•

Gwen Troake

MACDONALD AND JANE'S · LONDON

The following recipes have appeared elsewhere: Bramble Sauce, Spinach Pancakes with Cheese Sauce, Crab Pancakes, Salmon Pancakes, Chicken Pasty, Country Pasty, Apple Fluff, Favourite Fruit Cake, Fruit Bread and Chocolate Orange Cake in *Woman's Realm*; Minted Duckling, Baskets of Peas and Orange Salad, Devonshire Splits and Ginger Sponge Cake in *Woman*; and Sausage Rolls on *Wonderloaf* bread wrappers.

ISBN 0354 08513 1

First published in 1977 by Macdonald and Jane's (Publishers) Ltd, Paulton House, 8 Shepherdess Walk, London N1
Phototypeset by Trident Graphics Ltd, Reigate, Surrey
Printed and bound in Great Britain by
Redwood Burn Ltd, Trowbridge and Esher

Recipes are for four people, eggs are standard, and sugar granulated, unless otherwise stated.

Contents

Foreword

I first met Gwen Troake at the Cook of the Realm competition in 1972. She was one of the cooks and I was one of the judges. I soon discovered that judging was arduous work – I had to munch my way through two dozen exotic three-course meals. Soon I didn't care if I never saw another flambéd shrimp or pineappled ham. I was beginning to have real trouble forcing the tuna-fish titbits down, when at last I met Gwen – round and pretty as an apple dumpling, with a voice as sweet as Devonshire cream. The duck she cooked was crispy and delicious. Her pear meringues were delectable. She won, with an effortless flick of her spinach pancakes.

Half a dozen years later a programme called *The Big Time* was invented. It was a series of documentary films, each one offering a talented amateur a chance to try his or her skills in the professional world. For one programme, we decided to try and find an amateur cook, who could plan a banquet at the Dorchester Hotel. I remembered Gwen Troake, so we invited her to London to discuss the programme. And although she was against very strong competition (Britain seems to be crammed with brilliant housewife cooks, you lucky British husbands) once again Gwen proved irresistible. She is modest, humorous and kind – as full of goodness as her own marvellous country cooking. The programme was an uproarious success. It may seem immodest of me to say so – but then the success had very little to do with me. It was partly due to the fascination of seeing how a huge hotel kitchen works. It was partly the suspense of seeing whether Mr Edward Heath and Lord Mountbatten would enjoy the banquet Gwen had planned for them. It was largely due to the explosive confrontation between Gwen Troake and Fanny Cradock. Conversations between cooks often simmer quite hotly; this one boiled so dangerously that it provoked a wild correspondence in the national press, pro-Troake or pro-Cradock.

But the star attraction of the programme was Gwen, and Gwen's cooking. The programme began with Gwen making a potato pasty, in the farmhouse kitchen that used to belong to her mother. The recipe seemed to consist entirely of Devonshire cream, potatoes and buttery pastry – the table groaned under the delicious weight of calories. Gwen's friends had been invited for the traditional 'drinking time' – in Gwen's childhood it used to be a pasty and a jug of cider for the harvesters. These days in Gwen's kitchen it's saffron cakes and Devonshire splits, junket and scones, and cider cake with honey cream. All these recipes she has now collected in this book – and just to read them brings to the city gourmet the flavour of the Devon countryside, and traditional Devon cooking. Gwen doesn't scorn labour-saving ingredients, though. She is, after all, a busy farmer's wife who does her share of ploughing and harvesting. So these recipes are for any busy cook who loves the traditional taste of English cooking. And their success must be due to the discriminating palates of her husband Dudley, her daughters Teresa and Janet, and the artistry of the chef herself, Mrs Gwen Troake.

ESTHER RANTZEN

Gwen's
The Big Time Menu for
A Foyles Literary Lunch at
the Dorchester

Seafood Admiral

•

Roast Duckling with Bramble Sauce

•

Coffee Cream

Preparation: 15 min
Cooking: Simmer 15 min, 15 min at 450°F (230°C, Gas Mark 8)

8 oz (225 g) haddock
8 oz (225 g) whiting
½ oz (15 g) long-grain rice
¼ pt (150 ml) dry white wine

¼ pt (150 ml) water
2 tsp (30 ml) lemon juice
½ tsp (2.5 ml) salt
good pinch of pepper
1 oz (25 g) butter
1 oz (25 g) plain flour
milk
1 tbsp (15 ml) chopped parsley
4 oz (100 g) prawns
2 oz (50 g) cheese

Seafood Admiral

Remove skin from fish, slice into 1 in (2.5 cm) pieces, place in pan with rice, wine, water, lemon juice, salt and pepper. Bring to the boil, simmer for 15 min, then strain and reserve stock for sauce. Melt butter in pan, add flour, stir and cook gently for 2 min. Remove from heat and stir in ½ pt (300 ml) fish stock (make up quantity with milk if necessary). Return to heat and bring to the boil. Stir parsley, prawns, fish and rice into sauce, and pour into casserole. Sprinkle grated cheese over, bake until golden. (If liked, 8–12 scallops can be used to replace the haddock and whiting in this recipe.)

Preparation: 15 min
Cooking: 2½ hr at 350°F
(180°C, Gas Mark 4)

5 lb (2.3 kg) oven-ready
duckling
1 oz (25 g) butter
1 tbsp (15 ml) chopped
onion and parsley
½ tsp (2.5 ml) salt

Bramble Sauce

Preparation: 15 min
Cooking: 20 min

6 oz (175 g) blackberries
¾ pt (450 ml) water
2 tbsp (30 ml) cornflour
1 lemon jelly
2 tsp (10 ml) sugar
½ tsp (2.5 ml) salt
2 tbsp (30 ml) red wine

Roast Duckling with Bramble Sauce

Wash duckling inside and out, then leave to drain. Meanwhile cream butter and add chopped onion and parsley. Spread inside duckling. Make a 1 in (2.5 cm) slit just above vent and pull the tail through to prevent butter running out. Rub salt into duck skin. Place duck on rack in baking dish, breast down. Cook for 1 hr. Turn duck over on rack, breast up, and cook for a further 1½ hr or until crisp and golden brown and well cooked.

Bramble Sauce

Bring blackberries and water to boil, simmer for 15 min. Then put fruit and juice through a sieve. Blend cornflour with a little cool juice, put the remaining juice in a pan with the jelly squares, sugar and salt, heat until jelly dissolves, stir in cornflour. Bring to the boil and keep stirring until it clears. Add red wine.

Preparation: 20 min
Cooking: 10 min

7 oz (200 g) butter
1 oz (25 g) plain flour

¼ pt (150 ml) milk
4 tsp (20 ml) instant coffee
6 oz (175 g) castor sugar
1 packet of sponge fingers
4 tbsp (60 ml) sherry or rum
2 tbsp (30 ml) water

Coffee Cream

Slowly melt 1 oz (25 g) butter in saucepan, stir in flour and cook for 1 min, remove pan from heat and gradually add milk and instant coffee. Replace pan on heat and bring to the boil, stirring all the time. Cook gently for 2 min. Cool. Cream together sugar and remaining butter, add the cool coffee sauce a spoonful at a time and beat well. Mix rum and water. Put a layer of coffee cream into glass serving dish. Lightly dip eight sponge fingers in rum mixture and arrange in glass dish on coffee cream, repeat another layer of coffee cream and a layer of sponge fingers, finish with a layer of coffee cream and decorate top with walnuts and whipped cream. This is delicious served with fruit. There should be enough for 8 portions.

This is the lovely creamy pudding Mr. Heath didn't get. My family and friends all love it, especially with fruit, fresh or tinned.

14

A Harvest Supper

Baked Gammon
eaten cold with salads,
pickled beetroot and chutney

•

Peaches in Cider
with Devonshire Clotted Cream

•

Harvest Saffron Cake
with butter and cheese

Preparation: 5 min
Cooking: Simmer 1¾ hr,
  plus 50 min at 350°F
  (180°C, Gas Mark 4)

5 lb (2.3 kg) middle gammon
6 peppercorns
bunch mixed herbs
1 tsp (5 ml) dry mustard
4 tbsp (60 ml) brown sugar

Baked Gammon

Place gammon in bowl of cold water and soak overnight. Drain, and then put gammon in large saucepan with peppercorns and herbs, cover with fresh water and bring to the boil. Skim top, replace lid and continue simmering for 1¾ hr. Lift gammon out to drain and remove rind, then score fat into squares. Place gammon in baking dish, mix mustard with sugar and sprinkle over fat on gammon. Bake for 50 min basting often.

Preparation: 15 min
Cooking: 15 min at 350°F
(180°C, Gas Mark 4)

4 fresh peaches
4 digestive biscuits
3 oz (75 g) cream cheese
1 tbsp (15 ml) apple purée
1 tbsp (15 ml) double cream
¼ pt (150 ml) cider

Devonshire Clotted Cream

Preparation: 3 min
Cooking: 3–4 hr

4 pt (2.4 lt) new milk

Peaches in Cider

Skin peaches, cut in half and remove stone. Crush biscuits and rub through a sieve. Beat together cheese and apple purée, add cream, stir in sifted biscuits. Arrange peaches in casserole hollow side up, fill each cavity with mixture, either by piping or with a teaspoon. Pour cider around peaches and bake for 15 min or until nicely browned.

Devonshire Clotted Cream

Pour new milk into an enamel bowl, leave to stand in a cool place overnight. Place bowl over very low heat and leave until the surface has formed a crust. Remove from heat and stand in a cool place for at least 12 hr or preferably overnight. Carefully skim cream from the top of the milk.

Preparation: 20 min
Cooking: 15 min at 400°F
(200°C, Gas Mark 6) and
30 min at 350°F (180°C,
Gas Mark 4)

Ingredients for 3 cakes
2 packets saffron
2 oz (50 g) fresh yeast

1½ pt (900 ml) lukewarm
milk
1 lb (450 g) granulated sugar
3 lb (1.3 kg) plain flour
½ tsp (2.5 ml) salt
1 lb (450 g) margarine
12 oz (325 g) currants
12 oz (325 g) sultanas
2 oz (50 g) mixed peel

Harvest Saffron Cake

Snip up saffron and put in a basin with 3 tbsp (45 ml) of boiling water. Leave to soak overnight. Whisk yeast into lukewarm milk and add 2 tsp (10 ml) of the sugar and 4 oz (100 gm) of the flour. Mix all together and allow to 'sponge' in a warm place. Sift flour and salt into a large warm enamel pan or bowl. Rub in margarine. Mix in sugar, fruit and peel. Stir together saffron mixture and sponged yeast. Pour over ingredients in bowl and stir together thoroughly. Cover with a clean damp cloth and put in a warm place to rise. Place risen mixture in 3 large well-greased cake tins and allow to prove. When risen bake for 15 min at 400°F (200°C, Gas Mark 6), then reduce temperature to 350°F (180°C, Gas Mark 4) for a further 30 min, or until cooked.

A great favourite with family and friends.

Starters
and
Snacks

Preparation: 3 min

1 slice bread
boiling water
2 tbsp (30 ml) clotted cream
pinch of salt

Kettle Broth

Break bread into small pieces and place in bowl, cover with boiling water, drain off water, add cream and sprinkle on salt. Pepper may be added if desired. Serves one.

This is a traditional Devon breakfast dish, which used to be eaten instead of cereal, or as a substitute for early morning tea and biscuits. It was usually followed by bacon and eggs.

Preparation: 20 min
Cooking: 15 min

4 large eggs
1 lettuce
6 tbsp (90 ml) mayonnaise
1 tbsp (15 ml) tomato
    ketchup

6 oz (175 g) prepared
    prawns
small tin of sardines
4 tbsp (60 ml) cockles in
    vinegar
16 mussels in vinegar
paprika pepper
4 lemon wedges

Fisherman's Egg Mayonnaise

Place eggs in saucepan, cover with cold water and bring to the boil. Simmer for 8 min, remove from heat and place immediately in cold water, then remove shells. Wash, drain and dry lettuce. Mix together mayonnaise and ketchup. Arrange lettuce leaves on four plates. Cut each egg in half and place on lettuce, cover with mayonnaise and sprinkle with paprika pepper. Arrange seafood around eggs. Serve with lemon wedges and thinly sliced brown bread and butter.

Shrimp and Prawn Stuffed Avocado Pears

Preparation: 15 min

2 tbsp (30 ml) mayonnaise
1 tbsp (15 ml) tomato
　ketchup
1 tbsp (15 ml) double cream
pinch of salt
large pinch of pepper
3 oz (75 g) prepared prawns
3 oz (75 g) prepared shrimps
2 avocado pears
1 tbsp (15 ml) lemon juice
1 oz (25 g) smoked salmon

Fish Flan

Preparation: 15 min
Cooking: 40 min at 400°F
　(200°C, Gas Mark 6)
tin of sardines
2 oz (50 g) peeled prawns
4 oz (100 g) sliced tomato
3 eggs
large pinch each of salt and
　pepper
6 fl oz (180 ml) single cream
2 oz (50 g) grated onion
3 oz (75 g) grated cheese

Shrimp and Prawn Stuffed Avocado Pears

Place in bowl mayonnaise, ketchup, cream, salt and pepper, mix together and fold in prawns and shrimps. Cut pears in half lengthways with a stainless steel or silver knife, twist apart and remove stone, sprinkle each half with lemon juice. Divide prawn mixture into the pear halves. Top with flakes of smoked salmon.

Fish Flan

Mash sardines and spread on base of cooked flan case (see page 110). Scatter prawns and arrange tomato slices on top. Beat eggs in basin, add cream, onion, cheese, salt and pepper. Spoon over tomato slices. Bake for 40 min or until firm.

Ham Toasties
Preparation: 15 min
Cooking: 2–3 min

4 slices of toast
4 slices of ham
4 pineapple rings
3 oz (75 g) grated cheese
2 oz (50 g) butter

Melon with Stem Ginger Slices

Cut melon into four wedges and scoop off the seeds. Run a sharp knife between melon skin and flesh, and cut each wedge into six chunks. Slice ginger thinly, and place one slice between each of the melon chunks. If liked, a little of the syrup from the preserved ginger may be poured over each melon portion.

Ham Toasties

Butter toast. Place a slice of ham on each piece of toast. Top with a pineapple ring. Sprinkle with grated cheese. Place under a preheated grill for 2–3 min or until cheese melts to a golden brown.

Preparation: 15 min
Cooking: 15 min at 400°F
  (200°C, Gas Mark 6)

5 oz (125 g) plain flour
salt
pepper
1 large egg
¾ pt (450 ml) milk

¼ pt (150 ml) water
1 oz (25 g) lard
1 tbsp (15 ml) chopped
  parsley
7½ oz (210 g) tin red salmon
1 oz (25 g) butter
2 oz (50 g) Cheddar cheese
½ oz (15 g) Parmesan
  cheese

Salmon Pancakes

Sift 4 oz (100 g) flour with a pinch of salt and pepper, make a well in the centre and break in egg. Mix ¼ pt (150 ml) milk with ¼ pt (150 ml) water, add half of this to flour and beat until smooth, then add remaining milk and water. Heat lard in frying pan, pour off excess, then pour in enough batter to cover base of pan. Cook for 1 min or until underside is golden, then turn over and cook the other side. Make five more pancakes and keep hot. Grate Cheddar cheese, drain salmon and flake flesh. Melt 1 oz (25 g) butter in saucepan and stir in 1 oz (25 g) flour, then cook for 2 min over gentle heat. Take off heat and gradually stir in the remaining ½ pt (300 ml) milk. Return to heat and bring to the boil, stirring, then cook for 2 min on gentle heat. Remove from heat and stir in the Cheddar cheese. Season with salt and pepper. Take half the sauce and stir in the salmon and chopped parsley. Put some of this mixture on each pancake, roll up and arrange side by side in a casserole. Pour the rest of the sauce over the pancakes and then sprinkle Parmesan cheese on top. Put the dish in the centre of a preheated oven and bake for 15 min or until sauce is bubbling. Garnish with sprigs of parsley.

Preparation: 15 min
Cooking: 20 min at 375°F
 (190°C, Gas Mark 5)

5 oz (125 g) plain flour
½ tsp (2.5 ml) salt
1 pt (600 ml) milk
1 egg
2 oz (50 g) butter
4 oz (100 g) grated cheese
8 oz (225 g) cooked spinach
½ tsp (2.5 ml) grated
 nutmeg
large pinch of pepper
fat for frying

Spinach Pancakes with Cheese Sauce

Sift 4 oz (100 g) flour with ¼ tsp salt. Make a batter by beating egg, and adding to sifted flour with ½ pt (300 ml) milk, a little at a time. (Makes six pancakes.) Fry in hot butter, then keep hot. Stir nutmeg and pepper into spinach and make layers of pancakes and spinach in baking dish. Make sauce by melting 1 oz (25 g) butter, add 1 oz (25 g) sifted flour and remaining salt, stir and cook for 2 min. Take off heat and stir in ½ pt (300 ml) milk, return to heat and bring to the boil, stirring all the time. Cook for 2 min, fold in 3 oz (75 g) grated cheese. Pour over pancakes and top with remaining cheese. Dot with butter and bake until golden.

This was my starter for the 1972 'Cook of the Realm' and won first prize. I also had the pleasure of meeting Esther Rantzen for the first time.

Crab Pancakes
Preparation: 15 min
Cooking: 15 min at 400°F
(200°C, Gas Mark 6)

4 oz (100 g) plain flour
pinch of salt and pepper
1 large egg
¼ pt (150 ml) milk
¼ pt (150 ml) water
1 oz (25 g) lard
4 oz (100 g) fresh cooked
  crab meat
5 oz (125 g) mayonnaise
½ cucumber

Raw Potato Fry
Preparation: 20 min
Cooking: 20 min

2 lb (900 g) potatoes
4 oz (100 g) onions
2 oz (50 g) dripping
1 tsp (5 ml) salt
good pinch of pepper
1½ pt (900 ml) cold water
4 large eggs
8 bacon rashers

Crab Pancakes

Make up pancakes as described for salmon pancakes (page 24) and keep hot. Flake the crab meat, chop the cucumber and add the mayonnaise; mix together. Spoon some of the mixture on each pancake and roll up. Serve immediately, or put in a casserole and heat in centre of preheated over for 15 min. (You could also add a sauce made of condensed tomato soup – just pour into dish with pancakes before heating it through in the oven.)

Raw Potato Fry

Peel and thinly slice potatoes and onions. Melt dripping in pan, add potato, onion, salt, pepper and cold water. Place on heat and bring to the boil. Simmer for 15 min or until cooked. Meanwhile fry bacon and eggs, and keep hot. Transfer potato mixture to frying pan, and 'crisp' for a few minutes over medium heat. (Potato will then be flavoured by bacon fat.) Serve immediately with the bacon and eggs.

Preparation: 15 min
Cooking: 20 min at 450°F
   (230°C, Gas Mark 8)

5 oz (125 g) plain flour

1 tsp (5 ml) salt
4 oz (100 g) butter
3 oz (75 g) sultanas
1 lb (450 g) mashed potato
1 egg

Potato Cakes

Sift flour with salt into bowl and rub in butter; then stir in sultanas and mashed potato with the hand. Roll out on a floured board and cut out 16 rounds with a 3 in (7.5 cm) cutter. Beat the egg, and brush the top of each cake. Arrange cakes on a baking tray and bake for 20 min or until golden brown. Serve with butter.

Preparation: 25 min
Cooking: 1¼ hr at 350°F
    (180°C, Gas Mark 4)

8 oz (225 g) self raising flour
2 oz (50 g) butter

2 oz (50 g) lard
3 tbsp (45 ml) cold water
1 lb (450 g) potatoes
4 tbsp (60 ml) clotted cream
large pinch of salt
large pinch of pepper
1 egg

West Country Potato Pasty

Sift flour with pinch of salt, and rub in butter and lard. Make into a dough with the water, then rest in refrigerator for about ten minutes. Peel potatoes and slice thinly. Roll out half the pastry on a floured board and line an 8 in (20 cm) pie plate. Fill with half of the sliced potato, spoon on cream and sprinkle on a pinch of salt and pepper, then top with remaining potatoes. Roll out the other pastry half for a lid. Damp pasty edge with water, then place on lid and press edges to seal. Brush top with beaten egg and prick with a fork, then bake until golden brown. Eat hot with gammon and homemade chutney. Serves 6.

Chef Kaupler at the Dorchester Hotel tasted this and liked it, He opened a bottle of Champagne to go with it

Chipple Pasty

Preparation: 20 min
Cooking: 1 hr at 350°F
   (180°C, Gas Mark 4)

Pastry as for potato pasty
  (see recipe page 28)
6 oz (175 g) 'chipples' (the
  young green tops from
  shallots)
¼ pt (150 ml) double cream
large pinch of salt
large pinch of pepper
beaten egg for glaze

Sausage Rolls

Preparation: 15 min
Cooking: 10 min at 425°F
  (220°C, Gas Mark 7)

12 slices of bread
6 oz (175 g) cheese
6 oz (175 g) butter
1 tsp (5 ml) made mustard
12 cooked sausages

'Chipple' Pasty

Wash 'chipples', drain and dry. Cut into ½ in (1 cm) lengths. Line a pie plate with pastry. Place half of the 'chipples' in pie plate. Pour on the cream and sprinkle with salt and pepper. Put remaining 'chipples' on top. Roll out pastry for lid. Dampen edges on both pie and lid, then press together for a good seal. Brush lid with beaten egg and make 3 slits in it to enable steam to escape. Bake for 1 hr. Makes one large pasty for 6 people.

Sausage Rolls

Trim crusts off bread. Grate cheese and mix with butter and mustard. Spread half the mixture on slices of bread, place a sausage on each slice and roll up. Top each sausage roll with the remaining mixture and place on a greased tray. Bake for 10 min or until golden brown.

This recipe appeared on eight million bread wrappers.

Preparation: 20 min

1 large Hovis loaf
4 oz (100 g) butter
½ tsp (2.5 ml) mint jelly
½ tsp (2.5 ml) salt
large pinch of pepper
¼ tsp (1.25 ml) made
 mustard

8 cooked duck slices
4 lettuce leaves
12 cucumber slices
12 tomato slices
12 orange segments
4 prunes
1 tbsp (15 ml) grated cheese
4 radishes
French dressing

Duckling Sandwiches

Cut eight slices of bread and finely trim crusts. Mix together butter, mint jelly, salt, pepper and mustard. Spread on bread. Divide duck between four of the buttered bread slices, then sandwich together with remaining four. Spread more of butter mixture on top of each sandwich and cover with a lettuce leaf. Then place alternately three slices of cucumber, three slices of tomato and three orange segments across lettuce, to make a diagonal row. Remove stones from prunes and stuff with grated cheese. Place on sandwich and tuck a radish rose into each. Serve with French dressing. Sandwiches are best eaten immediately to obtain maximum flavour.

This won a sandwich competition in which there were 7,000 entries.

Main
Dishes

Preparation: 25 min
Cooking: 40 min at 400°F
(200°C, Gas Mark 6)

4 fresh trout
3 oz (75 g) cooked chicken

2 oz (50 g) breadcrumbs
1 tbsp (15 ml) chopped
parsley
2 tbsp (30 ml) single cream
pinch of pepper
½ tsp (2.5 ml) salt
1 oz (25 g) butter

Trout Stuffed with Chicken

Gut and clean fish leaving heads on. Wash well in cold running water, drain and wipe dry. Mince cooked chicken, add breadcrumbs, parsley, cream, pepper and half the salt, mix together thoroughly, divide into four portions and stuff trout. Melt butter and add the rest of salt and pinch of pepper; brush on to fish. Place each trout separately in foil to make four neat parcels, place on baking tray and bake.

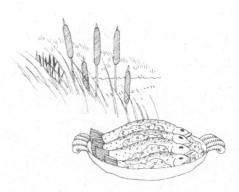

Preparation: 15 min
Cooking: 45 min at 350°F
(180°C, Gas Mark 4)

8 oz (225 g) cod
8 oz (225 g) haddock
1 tbsp (15 ml) chopped
parsley

1 tbsp (15 ml) chopped
onion
¼ pt (150 ml) milk
4 tbsp (60 ml) single cream
½ tsp (2.5 ml) salt
good pinch of pepper
3 oz (75 g) self raising flour
1½ oz (40 g) butter
2 oz (50 g) cheese

Fish Crumble

Remove skin from fish and cut into 1 in (2.5 cm) pieces, then place in alternate layers in pie dish with onion and parsley. Mix milk, cream, salt and pepper together and pour over fish mixture. Make crumble by rubbing butter into flour, stir in the grated cheese. Sprinkle crumble on top of the fish in dish and bake until golden and cooked.

Preparation: 15 min
Cooking: 30 min at 350°F
   (180°C, Gas Mark 4)

4 herrings
2 oz (50 g) brown
   breadcrumbs
1 cooking apple
1 onion
1 tbsp (15 ml) chopped
   parsley
½ tsp (2.5 ml) salt
good pinch of pepper
1 oz (25 g) butter

Stuffed Herrings

Cut heads off fish, scrape away scales. Take out roe and clean each herring thoroughly without slitting underside. Peel and grate apple and onion, mix with breadcrumbs, parsley, salt and pepper, stuff fish. Arrange in greased pie dish head to tail, dot with butter and cover with greased paper, bake in moderate oven.

Another method of stuffing herrings is to remove backbone. Proceed as before and clean herring, then slit underside, place fish skin uppermost on board and press hard along backbone, turn fish over and take out backbone by starting at the head end. Leave tail on but cut off fins. Spread with stuffing and roll up herring starting at the head end. Arrange in greased pie dish, dot with butter, cover with greased paper and bake.

Preparation: 35 min
Cooking: 1½ hr at 325°F
(170°C, Gas Mark 3), 40
min at 425°F (220°C, Gas
Mark 7)

8 oz (225 g) flaky pastry *(see
recipe page 108)*

1½ lb (675 g) beef steak
8 oz (225 g) kidney
4 oz (100 g) mushrooms
½ pt (300 ml) stock
1 oz (25 g) flour
½ tsp (2.5 ml) salt
large pinch of pepper
1 egg

Steak and Kidney Pie

Cut steak and kidney in thin slices. Place a slice
of kidney on a slice of steak and roll up. Arrange
meat in pie dish, and sprinkle each layer with
flour, salt and pepper. Fix pie funnel in centre,
pour on stock, cover with foil and simmer in
oven for 1½ hr. Meanwhile make pastry and rest
in refrigerator. Chop mushrooms. Remove pie
from oven and add mushrooms. Roll out pastry
on floured surface about ½ in (1 cm) larger than
dish, trim off ½ in (1 cm) strip and place on
dampened dish edge. Brush strip with water and
fix lid, press edges with fork to seal. Brush with
beaten egg and bake until golden brown.

Preparation: 20 min
Cooking: 15 min plus 2 hr at
325°F (170°C, Gas Mark 3)

1½ lb (675 g) lean braising
steak
2 oz (50 g) butter
1 onion
1 cooking apple

1 tbsp (15 ml) curry powder
1 tbsp (15 ml) plain flour
¾ pt (450 ml) stock
1 tbsp (15 ml) mango
chutney
1 tbsp (15 ml) lemon juice
2 oz (50 g) sultanas
large pinch of salt
large pinch of pepper

Mild Beef Curry

Cut meat into 1 in (2.5 cm) cubes, place in
casserole. Peel and slice onion and apple, fry in
butter for 3–4 min, stir in curry powder. Cook
gently for 5 min, then stir in flour and stock and
bring to the boil. Add chutney, lemon juice and
sultanas, and season with pepper and salt. Pour
curry sauce over beef in casserole, cover with
lid and cook slowly for 2 hr.

Preparation: 30 min
Cooking: Simmer 1 hr.
30–35 min at 400°F
(200°C, Gas Mark 6)

1½ lb (675 g) topside
2½ oz (60 g) lard
7 oz (200 g) self raising or
plain flour

1 beef stock cube
1 pt (600 ml) hot water
salt and pepper
1 bay leaf
good pinch of mixed herbs
1½ oz (40 g) margarine
7½ oz (215 g) puff pastry
(see recipe page 111)
1 standard egg yolk

Country Pasty

Cut the meat into 2 in (5 cm) strips, discarding excess fat. Fry the meat in 1 oz (25 g) lard until browned, stir in 1 oz (25 g) flour and cook until it is absorbed. Dissolve stock cube in hot water, add to meat in pan with bay leaf and herbs, season with salt and pepper, bring to the boil and simmer for 1 hr, or until meat is tender. Leave meat to cool, then drain off surplus gravy and discard bay leaf. Sift the rest of the flour with a good pinch of salt, rub in the margarine and remaining 1½ oz (35 g) lard until mixture resembles fine breadcrumbs. Mix to a stiff dough with cold water. Roll out dough to a 9 in (23 cm) circle and put on a baking tray. Place meat on pastry, leaving 2 in (5 cm) clear all round the edge. Brush edge with water, roll out the puff pastry to a 9 in (23 cm) circle and put on top of the meat. Seal the pastries together at the edges. Use any trimmings to make leaves for the top. Brush with beaten egg, make 2 slits in the top of the pastry to enable steam to escape, and bake in the centre of a preheated oven for 30–35 min or until golden.

Preparation: 15 min
Cooking: 1 hr 20 min at
   425°F (220°C, Gas Mark
   7)

10 oz (280 g) flaky pastry
   (see recipe page 108)
2 lb (900 g) fillet of beef
2 oz (50 g) fat
4 oz (100 g) button mush-
   rooms
large pinch of salt
large pinch of pepper
1 egg

Preparation: 15 min
Cooking: 40 min at 400°F
   (200°C, Gas Mark 6)

Make flan case and bake
   blind *(see recipe page 110)*
3 oz (75 g) cooked ham
2 oz (50 g) grated onion
3 oz (75 g) grated cheese
3 eggs
large pinch of salt and
   pepper
¼ pt (150 ml) single cream
1 sliced tomato

Beef and Mushrooms in Pastry

Melt fat in baking dish, quickly seal beef on all sides in hot fat. Then roast for 40 min, lift out and allow to cool. Using two-thirds of the pastry, roll out on a floured surface into a rectangle 12 in by 18 in (30 cm by 45 cm). Place prepared mushrooms in centre of pastry, sprinkle with salt and pepper, place fillet on top of mushrooms, bring pastry up sides, and then roll out remaining third to fit top. Brush edges with water and place on top of fillet, seal edges, decorate with pastry leaves. Brush with beaten egg, place on damp baking tray and bake for 40 min or until pastry is golden brown. Serves 6–8.

Country Flan

Chop ham and spread over base of flan case. Beat eggs, then add cream, onion, cheese, salt and pepper. Spoon over ham. Arrange sliced tomato on top. Bake for 40 min or until firm.

Preparation: 35 min
Cooking: 2¼ hr

1½ lb (675 g) chuck steak
1½ oz (40 g) flour
pinch of salt
pinch of pepper
8 oz (225 g) onions
8 oz (225 g) carrots
2 oz (50 g) dripping
1¼ pt (750 ml) stock
8 oz (225 g) peeled potatoes
4 oz (100 g) sliced swede

Dough Boys

6 oz (175 g) self-raising flour
pinch of salt
3 oz (75 g) shredded suet
cold water

Beef Stew with Dough Boys

Cut the beef into ½ in (1 cm) cubes. Mix flour with the salt and pepper. Coat the beef with seasoned flour. Peel and slice onions and carrots. Melt dripping in a large pan. Place onions and beef into the hot fat for a few minutes and keep them moving around. Stir in the stock and bring to the boil, then add the carrots and season to taste. Simmer for 1½ hr. Add potatoes and swede. Bring to the boil and top with the dough boys. Simmer for a further 20 min.

Dough Boys

Sift flour and salt in mixing bowl. Mix in suet. Stir in enough water to make a stiff dough. Knead lightly and form into 12 balls, then place in stew and cook as instructed above.

My mother used to make dough boys with her stews — chicken, lamb and rabbit.

Preparation: 20 min
Cooking: 35 min at 375°F
   (190°C, Gas Mark 5)
1 large onion
3 oz (75 g) butter
1 oz (25 g) flour
½ pt (300 ml) stock
1 lb (450 g) minced cooked
   beef

8 oz (225 g) tin of baked
   beans
large pinch pepper
½ tsp (2.5 ml) salt
1 tbsp (15 ml)
   Worcestershire Sauce
1 lb (450 g) cooked mashed
   potatoes

Cottage Pie

Peel, chop and fry onion in 1 oz (25 gm) butter until tender. Remove from pan. Add flour and brown, gradually stir in stock and bring to the boil. Simmer for 1 min. Stir in onion, beef, beans and Worcestershire Sauce, season with salt and pepper. Put into a pie dish and cover with mashed potato. Dot top with remaining butter and bake until brown (approximately 30 mins).

Preparation: 7 min
Cooking: 15 min

1 lb (450 gm) sausages
1 large onion
1 lb (450 g) lamb's liver
1 oz (25 g) flour
large pinch of salt
lalrge pinch of pepper
4 rashers of bacon
2 oz (50 g) dripping

Creamed Swede

Preparation: 5 min
Cooking: 25 min

1 medium sized swede
½ tsp (2.5 ml) salt
large pinch pepper
2 tbsp (30 ml) double cream

Ploughman's Grill

Grill sausages. Meanwhile peel and slice onion. Cut liver into thin slices and coat with seasoned flour. Fry bacon for 3–4 min, then remove from heat and keep hot. Add dripping to pan, fry onion until tender, then put with bacon. Add liver to pan and fry for 6–7 min, browning both sides. Serve on a bed of Creamed Swede.

Creamed Swede

Peel swede and cut into ½ in (1 cm) cubes. Boil in slated water for 25 min or until tender. Drain and mash, then stir in cream. Place in vegetable dish and sprinkle top with pepper. Serve with hot liver, bacon and sausages.

Preparation: 20 min
Cooking: 1¾ hr at 350°F
   (180°C, Gas Mark 4)

12 oz (325 g) lean lamb
1 small swede
8 oz (225 g) self raising flour

pinch of salt
2 oz (50 g) butter
2 oz (50 g) lard
3 tbsp (45 ml) cold water
4 tbsp (60 ml) clotted cream
1 egg
salt and pepper

Lamb and Swede Pasty

Cut lamb into ½ in (1 cm) pieces, peel swede and finely slice 4 oz (100 g) to use. Sift flour and salt into bowl, rub in butter and lard, mix to a dough with cold water. Roll out two-thirds of dough on a floured surface, and with this line an 8 in (20 cm) pie plate. Place 2 oz (50 g) sliced swede on pastry, and cover with the lamb pieces. Dot with cream and season with salt and pepper, then top with remaining sliced swede. Roll out one-third of pastry for lid, dampen edges and place lid on swede, pressing edges together for a good seal. Brush with beaten egg, make two slits in the top, and bake for 1¾ hr or until well done.

Preparation: 3 min
Cooking: 35 min at 375°F
(190°C, Gas Mark 5)

8 pork chops
fat for frying
½ tsp (2.5 ml) salt
good pinch of pepper

Pineapple Sauce
Preparation: 5 min
Cooking: 5 min

12 oz (325 g) tin of pineapple
1 tbsp (15 ml) cider
1 tbsp (15 ml) sugar
1 tbsp (15 ml) cornflour
¼ tsp (1.25 ml) ginger
pinch of salt

Baked Pork Chops with Pineapple Sauce

Heat fat in pan and fry chops for 1 min on each
side to seal in juices. Place in a baking dish,
sprinkle with salt and pepper, then cover with
buttered greaseproof paper. Bake for 35 min or
until well done. Serve with pineapple sauce.

Pineapple Sauce
Put in liquidizer pineapple, cider, sugar,
cornflour, ginger and salt; liquidize for 1 min.
Pour into saucepan, place over gentle heat and
gradually bring to the boil stirring all the time.
Boil until it clears, then serve.

Preparation: 20 min
Cooking: 2 hr at 350°F
  (180°C, Gas Mark 4)

6 chicken joints, approx
  8 oz (225 g) each
4 oz (100 g) mushrooms
2 oz (50 g) butter

2 oz (50 g) flour
½ pt (300 ml) milk
½ pt (300 ml) white wine
pinch of salt
large pinch of pepper
2 tbsp (30 ml) single cream
1 tbsp (15 ml) chopped
  parsley
4 oz (100 g) green grapes

Chicken with White Wine Sauce

Skin chicken joints and cut in half. Rinse
mushrooms, drain and chop. Place chicken and
mushrooms in baking dish. Melt butter in a
saucepan, stir in flour and cook for 1 min. Take
off heat, stir in milk and wine, then put back on
heat and bring to the boil, stirring all the time.
Boil for 1 min. Add salt, pepper, cream and
parsley, stir, and pour sauce over chicken.
Cover dish and bake for 1 hr 55 min. Meanwhile
wash grapes and remove pips. Stir into sauce
and cook for a further 5 min.

Preparation: 20 min
Cooking: 30 min at 400°F
(200°C, Gas Mark 6)

1 oz (25 g) butter
7 oz (200 g) plain flour
½ chicken stock cube
¼ pt (150 ml) boiling water
¼ pt (150 ml) milk

salt and pepper
2 oz (50 g) mushrooms
12 oz (375 g) cooked
    chicken
7 oz (200 g) tin of sweetcorn
1½ oz (40 g) margarine
1½ oz (40 g) lard
7½ oz (215 g) puff pastry
    (see recipe page 111)
1 standard egg yolk

Chicken Pasty

Dissolve stock cube in boiling water, wash and slice mushrooms, cut chicken into rough pieces, drain sweetcorn. Melt the butter in pan, stir in 1 oz (25 g) flour and cook gently for 2 min. Take off the heat, gradually stir in stock and milk, then bring slowly to the boil stirring all the time. Season with salt and pepper, stir in mushrooms, chicken and sweetcorn, then leave to cool. To make the shortcrust pastry base, sift remaining flour with a good pinch of salt, then rub in margarine and lard. Mix to a stiff dough with cold water, then roll out and line an 8 in (20 cm) pie plate. Arrange chicken mixture on pastry and brush round edge with water, then roll out puff pastry for lid and place on top of chicken. Press edges together to seal, make leaves out of pastry trimmings for top of pastry, brush with beaten egg. Make two slits in the top. Bake in centre of preheated oven for 30 min or until golden.

Preparation: 15 min
Cooking: 1½ hr at 400°F
(200°C, Gas Mark 6)

3¼ lb (1.5 kg) chicken
4 oz (100 g) breadcrumbs
2 oz (50 g) chopped walnuts

1 tbsp (15 ml) chopped
parsley
½ tsp (2.5 ml) thyme
1 tsp (5 ml) lemon juice
1 egg
salt and pepper
1 oz (25 g) butter

Roast Chicken with Walnut Stuffing

Wash, drain and dry chicken. Make stuffing by mixing breadcrumbs, walnuts, parsley and thyme together; season with salt and pepper. Beat egg and add to stuffing with lemon juice. Stuff chicken. Melt butter and brush on to bird. Place on rack in roasting dish, then cook back upwards for ¾ hr. Turn, and with breast side upwards continue roasting for ¾ hr, or until cooked through. Make gravy with giblet stock. (Potatoes may be roasted in dish underneath chicken.)

Preparation: 15 min
Cooking: 10 min

1 lb (450 g) cooked turkey
1 lb (450 g) cooked potato
2 oz (50 g) suet
2 tbsp (30 ml) sage and
   onion stuffing

2 tsp (10 ml) chopped
   parsley
2 eggs
pinch of salt
pinch of pepper
breadcrumbs
4 oz (100 g) lard

Turkey Rissoles

Mince turkey, mash potato, then mix together
with suet, stuffing, parsley, salt and pepper.
Beat 1 egg and stir into mixture, shape into 12
rissoles. Beat remaining egg and dip each rissole
in it, then roll in breadcrumbs. Fry rissoles in
hot lard until golden brown, about 5 min each
side.

Preparation: 25 min
Cooking: 20 min per lb at
400°F (200°C, Gas Mark
6)

1 small goose, approx
6–10 lb (2.7–4.5 kg)

4 onions
4 oz (100 g) butter
4 oz (100 g) breadcrumbs
2 tsp (10 ml) sage
½ tsp (2.5 ml) salt
large pinch of pepper
1 tbsp (15 ml) single cream

Michaelmas Goose

Peel onions, cover with water in a saucepan, and bring to boil. Simmer for 10 min, then drain and mince onions. Place in bowl with 1 oz (25 g) butter, breadcrumbs, sage, salt, pepper and cream. Mix thoroughly with the hand. Put stuffing into prepared goose, and stitch up vent. Prick goose all over. Weigh goose and allow 20 min per lb for roasting, then brush with melted butter. Place on rack in baking dish back upwards for half the cooking time (baste every 30 min during cooking period). Turn goose and cook breast upwards for remaining time. Test to make sure it is well done by piercing thick part of leg with skewer. If juices run red, goose is not yet cooked. Serve with bramble sauce. (See page 13.)

Preparation: 25 min
Cooking: 2 hr at 350°F
(180°C, Gas Mark 4)

4 pigeons
2 onions

1 lb (450 g) cooking apples
8 oz (225 g) butter
¼ pt (150 ml) single cream
2 tbsp (30 ml) lemon juice
4 tbsp (60 ml) cider
large pinch of pepper
large pinch of salt

Pigeons in Cider

Wash and thoroughly clean birds, drain and dry. Heat 4 oz (100 g) butter in pan and brown pigeons on both sides. Peel and slice onions and apple, fry in remaining butter for 5 min. Put half of the apple and onion in bottom of deep baking dish, place pigeons on top and surround with remaining apple and onion. Mix cream with lemon juice, cider, salt and pepper, pour over birds. Cover with foil and cook for 2 hr or until tender.

Preparation: 20 min
Cooking: 1 hr at 400°F
   (200°C, Gas Mark 6)

1 pheasant
3 oz (75 g) minced beef
1 oz (25 g) suet

1 oz (25 g) chopped mush-
   rooms
1 tbsp (15 ml) chopped
   parsley
½ tsp (2.5 ml) salt
large pinch of pepper
1 tbsp (15 ml) brandy
4 rashers fat bacon

Roast Pheasant with Brandy Stuffing

Wash and drain pheasant in colander. Make stuffing by mixing together in bowl minced beef, suet, mushroom, parsley, salt, pepper and brandy. Place stuffing inside bird and stitch up vent (if too much stuffing has been made place remainder in small greased baking dish, cover with foil and bake separately in oven). Put pheasant in baking dish, cover well with slices of fat bacon (not too salty), pour a little water in dish and roast for 1 hr or until tender. (A large cock pheasant will feed up to four people, but the smaller hen pheasant only two to three.)

Preparation: 30 min
Cooking: 1¼–1¾ hr at 350°F
 (180°C, Gas Mark 4)

2 young rabbits
3 onions

2 oz (50 g) butter
4 oz (100 g) breadcrumbs
2 tsp (10 ml) sage
8 fat bacon slices
large pinch of pepper
pinch of salt

Roast Rabbit with Stuffing

Wash and clean rabbits, put to soak in salted water for 30 min, wipe and dry thoroughly. Chop onions and put in a bowl with butter, breadcrumbs, sage, salt and pepper. Mix together with the hand. Fill cavity in each rabbit with stuffing and sew up, then place in roasting tin. Cover completely with bacon slices, cook until well done.

Preparation: 30 min
Cooking: Simmer 1 hr. Bake
   40 min at 425°F (220°C,
   Gas Mark 7)

1 young rabbit
8 oz (225 g) streaky bacon
1 onion
1½ pt (900 ml) stock

1½ oz (40 g) plain flour
1½ oz (40 g) butter
large pinch of pepper
1 tbsp (15 ml) chopped
   parsley
2 tbsp (30 ml) single cream
8 oz (225 g) flaky pastry *(see
   recipe page 108)*
1 egg

Rabbit Pie

Cut rabbit into joints and soak in salted water
for 2½ hr, drain and dry. Slice bacon into 1 in
(2.5 cm) strips, slice onion and put in pan with
joints and stock, simmer for 1 hr or until tender.
Remove rabbit, onion and bacon from pan and
place in pie dish, with pie funnel in centre. Melt
butter in saucepan, stir in flour and cook gently
for 2 min. Add ¾ pt (450 ml) rabbit stock and
bring to the boil, stirring. Cook for 2 min, then
stir in parsley, pepper and cream. Pour sauce
over rabbit. Roll out pastry and make lid to fit
dish. Place a pastry strip round edge of dish,
brush with water and fit lid, trim and press edges
together with fork to seal. Brush with beaten egg
and decorate with pastry leaves, then bake pie
for 40 min or until golden brown.

Preparation: 30 min
Cooking: Simmer 3 hr 15
   min

1 hare
3 oz (75 g) plain flour
½ tsp (2.5 ml) salt
½ tsp (2.5 ml) pepper

4 oz (100 g) streaky bacon
4 onions
8 cloves
1½ pt (900 ml) stock
2 tsp (10 ml) lemon juice
4 tbsp (60 ml) port
bunch of mixed herbs
2 oz (50 g) cooking fat
redcurrant jelly

Jugged Hare

Cut hare into joints and soak in salted water for 30 min, drain and dry. Slice bacon into ½ in (1 cm) pieces and fry for 4–5 min, then remove from pan and add fat. Mix flour, salt and pepper, toss hare in mixture, then fry until brown on both sides. Put hare and bacon into heavy casserole, add onions spiked with cloves, lemon juice, port and herbs. Cover with stock, put on lid and simmer over low heat for 3 hr. Remove herbs, serve with redcurrant jelly.

Preparation: 20 min
Cooking: 25 min at 425°F
   (220°C, Gas Mark 7), and
   1¾ hr at 375°F (190°C,
   Gas Mark 5)

5 lb (2.3 kg) shoulder of
   lamb
6 oz (175 g) salmon (fresh

or tinned)
2 oz (50 g) cheese
2 tbsp (30 ml) chopped
   parsley
2 oz (50 g) breadcrumbs
1 tbsp (15 ml) single cream
1 egg
½ tsp (2.5 ml) salt
large pinch of pepper

Salmon Stuffed Shoulder of Lamb

Ask your butcher to tunnel-bone the shoulder
for stuffing. Flake cooked or tinned salmon,
grate cheese and mix together, adding breadcrumbs, parsley, salt and pepper. Beat egg, and
add with cream to the salmon stuffing to bind
together. Fill cavity in lamb shoulder with
stuffing, fold over flap of meat and tie up with
string into a neat parcel to keep the stuffing in.
Put into baking dish and cook for 25 min at
425°F (220°C, Gas Mark 7) and then at a
reduced heat for 1¾ hr at 375°F (190°C, Gas
Mark 5) or until well done. Serve with bilberry
tartlets (see page 58).

Preparation: 30 min
Cooking: 4½ hr at 325°F
  (170°C, Gas Mark 3)

14 lb (6.3 kg) turkey
12 oz (325 g) pickled pear
1 bunch parsley

1 large onion
10 oz (280 g) breadcrumbs
1 tsp (5 ml) salt
1 tsp (5 ml) pepper
1½ lb (675 g) pork
  sausagemeat
2 tbsp (30 ml) cream
4 oz (100 g) butter

Turkey with Pear and Parsley Stuffing

Wash turkey inside and out, dry with a clean cloth. Chop pear, onion and parsley, and mix together. Place in mixing bowl breadcrumbs, thyme, ½ tsp (2.5 ml) salt and ½ tsp (2.5 ml) pepper. Stir together with the hand and add pear mixture, sausagemeat and cream. Place three-quarters of the stuffing in body cavity and sew up opening. Fill neck cavity with remaining stuffing. Melt butter, add remaining salt and pepper, and brush bird all over. Place turkey on rack in a roasting tin and cover with greased greaseproof paper. Cook for 4½ hr or until done. If turkey is browning too much, cover with extra greaseproof paper.

Preparation: 15 min

3 oranges
1 lettuce

6 tbsp (90 ml) olive oil
3 tbsp (45 ml) vinegar
½ tsp (2.5 ml) salt
good pinch of pepper
1 tsp (5 ml) sugar

Orange Salad

Peel oranges so that there is no pith or skin. (Pop the oranges into a bowl of boiling water for 3–4 min, drain, then peel; the skin and pith will come away cleanly.) Either divide in segments with a stainless steel knife or cut in slices. Wash and drain lettuce then arrange leaves on serving dish topped with orange segments or slices. Shake olive oil, vinegar, salt, pepper and sugar in a screw-top jar till well blended; pour over orange salad just before serving.

Preparation: 15 min
Cooking: 2½ hr at 350°F
(180°C, Gas Mark 4)

5 lb (2.3 kg) duckling

1 oz (25 g) butter
1 tbsp (15 ml) chopped fresh
mint
½ tsp (2.5 ml) salt
3 tomatoes

Minted Duckling

If using frozen duckling, thaw overnight at room temperature. Remove giblets and use for gravy or soup. Wash duckling quickly inside and out, leave in colander to drain. Meanwhile beat butter with chopped mint and when you are ready to cook the duckling place minted butter in the body cavity. Make 1 in (2.5 cm) slit on breast side just above the vent and pull the parson's nose through, so that the minted butter will not run out. Prick duck all over and rub salt into skin. Place rack in roasting tin and set duck on this, breast down. Cook for 1 hr. Turn duck over on rack and cook for further 1½ hr or until crisp and golden and cooked through. Serve garnished with halved tomatoes, prepared baskets of peas (see following page) and orange salad (see opposite).

Preparation: 15 min
Cooking: 10 min at 400°F
(200°C, Gas Mark 6)

8 oz (225 g) shortcrust
pastry *(see recipe page 109)*
1 lb (450 g) frozen peas
2 oz (50 g) butter
½ tsp (2.5 ml) salt
good pinch of pepper
1 tsp (5 ml) sugar

Bilberry Tartlets
Preparation: 15 min
Cooking: 10 min at 400°F
(200°C, Gas Mark 6)

8 oz (225 g) shortcrust
pastry *(see recipe page 109)*
bilberry jam

Baskets of Peas

Roll out pastry very thinly, cut in 3 in (7.5 cm) rounds to line 12 patty tins. Prick bases lightly with fork, and fill with baking beans. Roll out remaining pastry and cut into 12 x 4 in (10 cm) long strips for handles. (Make a few extra for 'spares' as they are very fragile.) Place these on a separate baking sheet, in horseshoe shapes. Rest pastry in refrigerator for 30 min. Bake tartlets and horseshoe strips in hot oven for 10 min or until cooked through. Remove baking beans from tartlets and return to oven for further 2–3 min. Meanwhile place frozen peas in a pan with butter, salt, pepper and sugar. Cover and cook gently until soft, lift out half the peas with a draining spoon and save for final garnish. Mash the remaining peas in pan to a purée, or use an electric liquidizer. Spoon purée into tartlet cases then top with reserved whole peas. Fix pastry handles on baskets.

Bilberry Tartlets
Make and bake as for 'Baskets of Peas' (above) but omit handles and fill with bilberry jam.

Puddings

Preparation: 40 min
Cooking: 30 min at 425°F
 (220°C, Gas Mark 7)

1 lb (450 g) flaky pastry *(see recipe page 108)*

8 oz (225 g) mincemeat
8 oz (225 g) sliced pears
milk to glaze
1 tbsp (15 ml) granulated
 sugar
1 tbsp (15 ml) icing sugar

Pear and Mincemeat Slice

On a lightly floured surface roll pastry out thinly to an oblong 24 in by 7 in (61 cm by 17.5 cm). Cut oblong in half, take one piece and fold in half lengthways, cut 2 in (5 cm) slits along folded edge about ½ in (1 cm) apart. Place plain oblong on damp baking tray, cover with mincemeat leaving 1 in (25 cm) clear all round. On top of mincemeat arrange pear slices. Brush edges of pastry with water and place the cut pastry on top, press edges together to seal. Brush with milk and sprinkle on sugar. Bake for 30 min or until golden brown. Dust with icing sugar. Serve with double cream.

Preparation: 35 min
Cooking: 15 min

12 oz (350 g) fresh
    strawberries
4 trifle sponge cakes
strawberry jam

4 tbsp (60 ml) brandy
1 tbsp (15 ml) icing sugar
1 pt (600 ml) milk
2 oz (50 g) castor sugar
1 packet of custard powder
6 oz (200 ml) double cream
½ tsp (2.5 ml) vanilla
    essence

Strawberry Trifle

Wash and dry strawberries, reserving eight large ones for decoration, slice the remainder. Split sponge cakes and spread with jam, sandwich together and cut into quarters. Place in a glass dish and soak with brandy. Put strawberry slices on top and sprinkle with icing sugar. Using milk, castor sugar and custard powder make custard as directed on packet, cool slightly and spoon over fruit. Leave in a cool place to set. Whip cream and essence until thick, then pipe or spoon into eight piles on trifle around edge of glass dish and top each with a strawberry.

Preparation: 15 min
Cooking: 30 min at 300°F
   (150°C, Gas Mark 2)

1 lb (450 g) rhubarb
1 tbsp (15 ml) lemon juice

¼ pt (150 ml) water
4 oz (100 g) granulated sugar
2 oz (50 g) castor sugar
2 eggs
4 sponge cakes
raspberry jam

Rhubarb Meringue

Cut rhubarb into 1 in (2.5 cm) pieces, put in pan with lemon juice, water and 2 oz (50 g) granulated sugar, gently stew until tender. Separate eggs and beat yolks. Strain and liquidize rhubarb, then add to beaten yolks. Stir together. Split sponge cakes, spread with jam and sandwich together. Cut each into four pieces, place in base of casserole, cover with rhubarb mixture. Make meringue by whisking egg whites until stiff, whisk in 2 oz (50 g) granulated sugar, lightly fold in 2 oz (50 g) castor sugar. Top pudding with meringue and bake for 30 min or until golden brown.

Prune Crunch

Preparation: 30 min
Cooking: 20 min

1 lb (450 g) prunes
2 pt (1.1 lt) cold water
1 orange jelly
1 oz (25 g) toasted coconut

Peach Fool

Preparation: 10 min

1 lb 13 oz (823 g) tin sliced
  peaches
10 fl oz (300 ml) double
  cream
1 tbsp (15 ml) icing sugar
1 tbsp (15 ml) peach brandy

Prune Crunch

Separate dried prunes and place in a bowl with the cold water to soak overnight. Put prunes and liquid in pan, bring to the boil, simmer for 15 min and drain. Put jelly pieces into a measuring jug and make up to ¾ pt (450 ml) with prune juice, stir to dissolve jelly. Remove stones from prunes and liquidize or mince fruit. Stir prunes and jelly together and pour into a wetted mould. Leave to set in a cool place. When set turn out on to serving plate and sprinkle with toasted coconut. Serve with cream. There should be enough for 6 people.

Peach Fool

Drain sliced peaches and liquidize to a purée. Whip together cream, sugar and brandy, fold in purée and spoon into individual glasses. Serve with brandy snaps.

Preparation: 20 min
Cooking: 30 min at 375°F
(190°C, Gas Mark 5)

6 oz (175 g) plain flour

pinch of salt
3 oz (75 g) butter
1 oz (25 g) sugar
1 egg
1 lb (450 g) rhubarb

Rhubarb Sheaves

Wipe rhubarb and cut into six 12 in (30 cm) lengths, each about 2 oz (50 g) in weight. Sift flour with salt, add butter and rub in, stir in sugar, add beaten egg and make into a dough. Roll out on a floured surface 13 in by 18 in (33 cm by 45 cm). Cut six strips 3 in (7.5 cm) wide off 13 in (33 cm) side. Place stick of rhubarb on strip of pastry, dampen edges with water, fold over and press edges together for a good seal. Arrange on baking tray and bake for 30 min. Before serving cut each one into four 'sheaves'. Serve with sugar and hot custard or thin cream.

Preparation: 20 min
Cooking: 45 min at 375°F
 (190°C, Gas Mark 5)
1 lb (450 g) gooseberries
3 tbsp (45 ml) granulated
 sugar

1 tbsp (15 ml) cornflour
6 oz (175 g) plain flour
pinch of salt
3 oz (75 g) butter
1 oz (25 g) castor sugar
1 egg

Gooseberry Tart

Top and tail gooseberries, wash and drain. Mix granulated sugar with cornflour. Sift flour with salt into a bowl, rub in butter with the fingertips to form crumbs, stir in castor sugar, add beaten egg and make into a dough. Roll out two-thirds of the pastry on a floured surface, line an 8 in (20 cm) pie plate. Fill with gooseberries, sprinkle on mixed sugar and cornflour. Roll out remaining pastry for lid, dampen edges and place pastry on top of gooseberries, pressing edges together for a good seal. Cut two slits in the top to allow steam to escape. Sprinkle top with extra granulated sugar, and bake until golden brown and fruit is cooked (approx 45 min). Serve hot or cold with cream.

Preparation: 30 min
Cooking: 15–20 min at 400°F
(200°C, Gas Mark 6)

3 oz (75 g) self raising flour
3 oz (75 g) castor sugar
3 eggs

1 block strawberry ice
cream
8 oz (225 g) strawberries
4 oz (100 g) double cream
1 oz (25 g) icing sugar
½ tsp (2.5 ml) lemon juice
redcurrant jelly

Strawberry Ice Cream Sponge

Whisk eggs and castor sugar in a warm bowl until thick and fluffy, then gradually fold in sifted flour. Pour mixture into two prepared 7 in (18 cm) sandwich tins and bake for 15–20 min or until done. Turn out and cool. Meanwhile, soften ice cream, wash and dry strawberries, slice half of them and stir into the softened ice cream. Line a 7 in (18 cm) sandwich tin with foil, fill with ice cream mixture and freeze. Whip together cream, icing sugar, and lemon juice until thick. Decorate top of one sponge with the cream and remaining whole strawberries. Spread jelly on the base of the other sponge, place set ice cream on jelly and top with the decorated layer.

Preparation: 15 min
Cooking: 15 min

4 sponge cakes
1 tbsp (15 ml) apple jelly
2 oranges
1 pt (600 ml) milk
1 packet of custard powder
2 oz (50 g) sugar
¼ pt (150 ml) whipping
  cream

Preparation: 20 min
Cooking: 45 min at 375°F
  (190°C, Gas Mark 5)

8 oz (225 g) blackcurrants
1 lb (450 g) apples
2 oz (50 g) soft brown sugar
4 oz (100 g) self raising flour
pinch of salt
2 oz (50 g) butter
1 oz (25 g) crushed
  cornflakes
2 oz (50 g) granulated sugar

Quick and Easy Sweet

Split sponge cakes and spread with apple jelly. Sandwich together. Cut each into quarters and place in glass dish. Squeeze juice from oranges and pour over sponge cakes. Make custard with milk, sugar and powder according to directions on packet, spoon over sponges, put in a cool place. Whip cream and pipe on top of custard.

Blackcurrant and Apple Crumble

Remove stalks from blackcurrants, wash and drain. Peel, core and slice apples. Mix fruit together with brown sugar, and place in baking dish. Make crumble by sifting flour and salt into mixing bowl, rub in butter with fingertips to form crumbs, stir in cornflakes and granulated sugar. Spread crumble over fruit in dish. Bake for 45 min or until brown and fruit is cooked. Serve with custard or cream.

Preparation: 30 min
Cooking: 40 min at 400°F
(200°C, Gas Mark 6)
1 quantity choux pastry (see
recipe page 109)
8 oz (225 g) fresh
strawberries

6 oz (175 g) double cream
1 tbsp (15 ml) icing sugar
1 tbsp (15 ml) Grand
Marnier
2 oz (50 g) chocolate
½ oz (12.5 gm) flaked
almonds toasted

Strawberry Ring

Grease and flour a baking tray. Mark an 8 in (20 cm) circle. Pipe choux pastry on marked circle. Cover with a deep roasting tin and bake for 40 min or until golden brown. Wash and drain strawberries. Whip cream with sugar and Grand Marnier. Cut the ring horizontally through the middle. Fill base of ring with sliced strawberries, pipe whipped cream on top and replace choux lid. Melt chocolate in basin over hot water and spoon over ring. Sprinkle flaked almonds on the top.

Preparation: 15 min
Cooking: 2 hr
4 oz (100 gm) self-raising
  flour
pinch of salt
½ tsp (2.5 ml) baking
  powder

3 oz (75 g) breadcrumbs
4 oz (100 g) shredded suet
2 oz (50 g) granulated sugar
4 oz (100 g) stoned raisins
1 egg
1 tbsp (15 ml) syrup
little milk

Figgy Duff

Have a large saucepan of boiling water ready.
Sift flour with salt and baking powder in bowl.
Mix in breadcrumbs, suet, sugar and raisins.
Beat egg and add with the syrup to the ingredients in the bowl. If necessary use a little milk
to make a soft dough. Wrap ball of dough in
greased paper and then in a greased pudding
cloth. Tie loosely but firmly. Place in the boiling
water and boil for 2 hr. Top up pan with boiling
water as necessary. Serve with cream and extra
syrup.

Preparation: 25 min

12 gingernut biscuits
2 oz (50 g) butter
2 oz (50 g) brown sugar
2 eggs separated

3 oz (75 g) castor sugar
1 orange
1 lemon
½ oz (12.5 g) gelatine
6 oz (175 g) cream cheese
¼ pt (150 ml) single cream

Orange and Lemon Cheesecake

Crush gingernut biscuits with rolling pin between layers of greaseproof paper. Place butter and sugar in pan over low heat and melt, then add biscuit crumbs and stir together. Put in base of flan dish and press down. Whisk egg yolks with sugar in bowl over pan of hot water until thick and creamy. Squeeze juice from fruit, pour half into a basin, add gelatine and stand in pan of hot water. Beat cheese into egg mixture, add remaining fruit juice, cream and gelatine. Whisk egg whites and fold in. Pour over biscuit base and put in a cool place to set. Decorate with fresh orange slices. (When in season, use fresh strawberry slices or whole fresh raspberries for decoration.)

Profiteroles

Preparation: 20 min
Cooking: 25 min at 400°F
  (200°C, Gas Mark 4)

2½ oz (65 g) plain flour
pinch of salt
¼ pt (150 ml) water
2 oz (50 g) butter
2 medium eggs
½ tsp (2.5 ml) vanilla
  essence
½ pt (300 ml) double cream
2 tbsp (30 ml) single cream
2 tbsp (30 ml) icing sugar

Chocolate Sauce

Preparation: 3 min
Cooking: 6 min

5 fl oz (150 ml) water
5 oz (125 g) plain chocolate
1 oz (25 g) sugar
1 oz (25 g) butter

Profiteroles

Sift flour and salt into basin and put in a warm place. Put water and butter in saucepan, bring to the boil and take off heat immediately, add warm flour all at once and beat well until mixture leaves the sides of pan. Cool slightly. Whisk eggs and add to the mixture with the essence, then beat the mixture thoroughly. Spoon mixture into a large piping bag with a ½ in (1 cm) nozzle and pipe out 24 choux buns on a greased and floured baking tray, or spoon on with a tea-spoon. Bake for 25 min or until crisp and golden brown. Whip creams and sugar together until thick, pipe cream into each bun through a small slit. Pile profiteroles on to a dish, and serve with a chocolate sauce.

Chocolate Sauce

Place water, chocolate and sugar in bowl over pan of hot water, and keep stirring until melted. Stir in butter. Serve with profiteroles, separately, or pour hot sauce over profiteroles immediately before serving.

Preparation: 10 min
Cooking: 15 min
3 oz (75 g) self raising flour
1 oz (25 g) ground almonds
pinch of salt
1 large egg
½ pt (300 ml) milk

oil for frying
4 oz (100 g) butter
2 oz (50 g) moist brown
  sugar
4 oz (100 g) sliced stem
  ginger
1 tbsp (15 ml) brandy

Almond Pancakes with Ginger & Brandy

Sift together flour, almonds and salt into bowl.
Make a well in centre and add egg and ¼ pt (150
ml) of milk. Beat together until smooth, then
gradually stir in remaining milk. Heat oil in pan
and fry eight pancakes, keep hot. In a saucepan
heat gently together butter and brown sugar until
melted, add stem ginger slices and brandy.
Spread a little of this mixture on each pancake
and roll up. If there is any mixture left over,
pour on top of rolled up pancakes to serve.

Preparation: 10 min
Cooking: 5 min

1 lb 4 oz (550 g) tin lychees
15½ oz (450 g) tin pears

1 tbsp (15 ml) arrowroot
1 tbsp (15 ml) sugar
4 tbsp (60 ml) champagne or
   white wine
3 bananas

Champagne Fruit Cocktail

Drain juice from tinned fruit and reserve. Mix arrowroot with sugar and 2 tbsp (30 ml) fruit juice. Place ½ pt (300 ml) juice in pan over gentle heat, bring up to the boil and stir in arrowroot. Keep stirring and boil for 1 min. Take off heat, stir in champagne or wine, cool. Slice pears and bananas, put in stem glasses with lychees and top with champagne mixture. (Extra fruit juice may be used instead of champagne or wine.) Serve immediately.

Preparation: 10 min
Cooking: 3–4 min at 425°F
  (220°C, Gas Mark 7)

2 egg whites
3½ oz (100 g) castor sugar
½ oz (15 g) ground almonds

¼ tsp (1.25 ml) almond
  essence
1 sponge flan case or pastry
  flan case *(see recipe page
  110)*
1 tin blackcurrant pie filling
1 block dairy ice cream

Almond and Blackcurrant Flan

Make meringue by whisking egg whites until
stiff, whisk in sugar, fold in almonds and
essence. Place flan case on a heatproof plate, fill
with blackcurrant pie filling, spoon on ice cream.
Using meringue, completely cover ice cream and
edge of flan. Put in preheated oven for 3–4 min
or until golden. To make a change, use cherry or
apricot pie filling instead of blackcurrant.

Preparation: 12 min
Cooking: 2–3 min

2 large grapefruit

1 block strawberry ice
  cream
2 egg whites
4 oz (100 g) castor sugar
1 tsp (5 ml) instant coffee

Grapefruit Meringue Cups

Cut each grapefruit in half, scoop out segments, remove pith and pips, chop segments and divide between the four grapefruit cups. Whisk egg whites until stiff. Whisk in half the sugar, then fold in the rest and the instant coffee. Place a portion of ice cream on top of each grapefruit half, then pipe on a generous whirl of coffee meringue to cover the ice cream completely. Place under preheated grill for 2–3 min or until golden brown.

Preparation: 30 min
Cooking: 1 hr at 375°F
(190°C, Gas Mark 5)
8 oz (225 g) shortcrust
pastry *(see recipe page 109)*
1 marrow
13¼ oz (370 g) tin of
pineapple pieces
1 oz (25 g) stem ginger
2 tsp (10 ml) stem ginger
syrup
2 tbsp (30 ml) sugar
½ tsp (2.5 ml) cinnamon
1 tbsp (15 ml) cornflour
2 oz (50 g) sultanas
a little milk

Marrow and Pineapple Pie

Remove rind and seeds from marrow, cut into thin slices about 1 in (2.5 cm) square. Place ½ lb (225 g) sliced marrow into pie dish, then add pineapple pieces and juice, cut ginger into thin slices and dot over pineapple. Spoon on ginger syrup. Mix together sugar, cinnamon and cornflour then sprinkle over pineapple, add sultanas. Cover with another ½ lb (225 g) of sliced marrow. Roll out pastry, a little larger than pie dish. Cut off ½ in (1 cm) strip, dampen edge of dish and press strip on to it, dampen strip and place lid on that, then press edges together to seal in juices. Brush lid with milk, make 3 slits in pastry top to enable steam to escape. Bake for 1 hr or until cooked.

Preparation: 30 min
Cooking: Simmer 10 min;
  2½–3 hr at 225°F (110°C,
  Gas Mark ¼)

4 egg whites
8 oz (225 g) castor sugar

4 fresh pears
4 oz (100 g) granulated sugar
¼ pt (150 ml) sherry
½ pt (300 ml) double cream
2 oz (50 g) icing sugar
½ tsp (2.5 ml) vanilla
  essence

Pear Blossom

Line a large baking tray or 2 small ones with greaseproof paper. Draw eight 3 in (7.5 cm) circles on paper, turn it over and brush with oil. Put egg whites in a dry clean bowl and whisk until very stiff, then whisk in half the castor sugar a little at a time. With a metal spoon fold in the remaining castor sugar. Put meringue in a piping bag with a large star tube, fill in circles on paper then pipe two layers around edge of each to build up sides. Place in a cool oven for 2½–3 hr or until dried out. Peel, core and slice pears. Put granulated sugar in pan with sherry and dissolve, add pear slices, bring up to the boil and simmer for 10 min, drain pears. Whip cream with icing sugar and essence until thick. When ready to serve arrange pear slices in meringue cases and top with the whipped cream.

Preparation: 10 min
Cooking: 15 min
1 lb 13 oz (823 g) tin of
  apricots
2 eggs
4½ oz (115 g) marshmallows

3 tbsp (45 ml) apricot
  brandy
½ oz (15 g) gelatine
5 fl oz (150 ml) double
  cream
6 glacé cherries

Apricot Mallow

Drain apricots, reserving juice; chop fruit and place in a glass serving dish. Separate eggs. Put marshmallows, brandy and egg yolks in a pan and place over a low heat. Whisk until marshmallows have melted. Remove from heat and stir in ¼ pt (150 ml) of apricot juice. Dissolve gelatine in 2 tbsp (30 ml) of heated apricot juice. Whisk egg whites and fold into mixture, lastly add gelatine stirring all the time. Pour over apricots in glass dish and chill. Decorate with whipped cream and cherries. A little castor sugar may be whipped with the cream.

Preparation: 25 min
Cooking: 15 min

1 lb (450 g) cooking apples
¼ pt (150 ml) sweet cider

6 oz (175 g) castor sugar
3 large eggs
1 tbsp (15 ml) powdered
  gelatine
¼ pt (150 ml) single cream

Apple Fluff

Peel, core and slice the cooking apples, put them in a pan with the cider and cook gently for 15 min or until very tender. Push through a sieve to make a purée, stir in 2 oz (50 g) sugar and leave to cool. Spread over the base of a serving dish. Separate the eggs, put the yolks in a basin with castor sugar, whisk until mixture is very thick and creamy. Put the gelatine and 3 tbsp (45 ml) cold water in a small basin, stand the basin in pan of hot water and stir until gelatine has dissolved. Whisk into the mixture, stir in the single cream. Whisk egg whites until stiff then fold into the mixture, spoon on top of the apple purée, leave in a cold place until firm. Serve with clotted cream.

Raspberry Cream

Preparation: 15 min

1 lemon
¼ pt (150 ml) single cream
¼ pt (150 ml) double cream
2 tbsp (30 ml) castor sugar
1 egg
12 oz (350 g) fresh or frozen
   raspberries

Redcurrant Crumble

Preparation: 15 min
Cooking: 45 min at 375°F
  (190°C, Gas Mark 5)

8 oz (225 g) fresh
   redcurrants
8 oz (225 g) fresh
   raspberries
2 oz (50 g) soft light brown
   sugar
2 oz (50 g) butter
4 oz (100 g) self raising flour
pinch of salt
2 oz (50 g) granulated sugar

Raspberry Cream

Grate rind of lemon and squeeze out juice.
Whisk single and double creams together with
lemon rind. Fold in 1 tbsp (15 ml) lemon juice
and castor sugar. Then whisk egg white and with
the raspberries fold into the creamy mixture.
Spoon into stemmed glasses and chill.

Redcurrant and Raspberry Crumble

Pick stalks off redcurrants, wash with raspberries and drain. Mix fruits together, put into
casserole with the brown sugar. Sift flour and
salt into bowl. Add the butter and rub with
fingertips to form crumbs, stir in the granulated
sugar. Sprinkle crumble over the fruit and bake
until fruit is cooked and top is golden brown:
approximately 45 min.

Preparation: 5 min
Cooking: 5 min

8 oz (225 g) tin of apricots
1 tbsp (15 ml) vinegar

1 tbsp (15 ml) sugar
1 tbsp (15 ml) cornflour
¼ tsp (1.25 ml) nutmeg
large pinch of salt

Apricot Sauce

Liquidize together for 1 min apricots, vinegar, sugar, cornflour, nutmeg and salt. Heat gently in saucepan and gradually bring to the boil, stirring all the time. Boil until mixture clears. (This sauce is delicious with roast meats and poultry.)

Rum Syrup

Preparation: 3 min
Cooking: 5 min

3 oz (75 g) butter
6 oz (150 g) soft brown
sugar
2 tbsp (30 ml) rum
1 tbsp (15 ml) water

Devonshire Junket

Preparation: 5 min
Cooking: 3–4 min

1½ pt (900 ml) new milk
3 oz (75 g) granulated sugar
¼ tsp (1.25 ml) grated
nutmeg
4 tsp (20 ml) rennet
4 oz (100 g) clotted cream

Rum Syrup

Melt butter over gentle heat. Add sugar, rum and water, stir until dissolved. (Brandy may be used instead of rum – either syrup is delicious with Christmas pudding.)

Devonshire Junket

Gradually heat milk to lukewarm over low heat. Stir in sugar until it dissolves. Pour mixture into glass serving dish and stir in grated nutmeg. Quickly stir in rennet and immediately place junket in refrigerator or a cool place to set. Top with spoonfuls of clotted cream and serve.

Mock Cream
Preparation: 10 min

4 oz (100 g) butter
4 oz (100 g) icing sugar
1 tsp (5 ml) vanilla essence
4 tbsp (60 ml) thick vanilla
   blancmange

Syllabub
Preparation: 15 min

½ pt (300 ml) double cream
4 oz (100 g) castor sugar
3 tbsp (45 ml) white wine
1 lemon

Mock Cream

Cream together butter and sifted sugar. Stir in essence. Add blancmange by the spoonful and beat well. Chill before serving.

Syllabub

Grate rind of lemon and squeeze out juice. Place in bowl cream, sugar, wine, lemon juice and grated rind. Whisk together until thick, put into individual glasses for serving. Chill well. Serve with brandy snaps or sponge fingers.

Preparation: 5 min
Cooking: 1½ hr at 325°F
(170°C, Gas Mark 3)

2 oz (50 g) macaroni
2 oz (50 g) sultanas
2 oz (50 g) sugar
1½ pt (900 ml) new milk

Macaroni Milk Pudding

Place macaroni in the bottom of a heatproof dish, scatter sultanas on top and sprinkle on sugar. Pour milk over, and bake for 1½ hr. (Rice pudding can be made in the same way, replacing the macaroni with rice.)

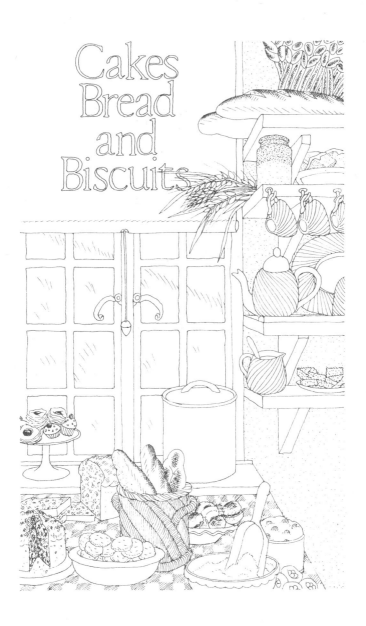

Cakes
Bread
and
Biscuits

Preparation: 30 min
Cooking: 1 hr at 325°F
(170°C, Gas Mark 3) and
1 hr at 300°F (150°C, Gas
Mark 2)

6 oz (175 g) self raising flour
4 oz (100 g) plain flour
large pinch of salt

2 oz (50 g) walnuts
2 oz (50 g) cherries
4 oz (100 g) butter
4 oz (100 g) margarine
8 oz (225 g) castor sugar
4 eggs
1 tsp (5 ml) almond essence
8 oz (225 g) currants
8 oz (225 g) sultanas
1 tbsp (15 ml) milk

Fruit and Nut Cake

Sift flours and salt into bowl. Chop nuts and cherries. Cream together butter, margarine and sugar. Beat eggs, add to the creamed mixture with a little of the flour. Stir in essence. Add the nuts and cherries and the remaining flour and fruit; mix well together. Add milk if mixture is not soft enough. Pour into a greased and lined 8½ in (21 cm) cake tin. Bake for 1 hr at 325°F (170°C, Gas Mark 3) and for a further 1 hr at 300°F (150°C, Gas Mark 2) or until cooked.

Preparation: 30 min
Cooking: 3 hr 15 min at 300°F (150°C, Gas Mark 2)

6 oz (175 g) plain flour
6 oz (175 g) self raising flour
large pinch of salt
1 lemon
6 oz (175 g) currants

6 oz (175 g) sultanas
6 oz (175 g) raisins
2 oz (50 g) mixed peel
2 oz (50 g) glacé cherries
9 oz (250 g) butter
9 oz (250 g) castor sugar
4 eggs
2 tbsp (30 ml) milk
6 oz (175 g) blanched almonds

Dundee Cake

Sift flour and salt together. Grate lemon. Pick over fruit and chop cherries. Cream butter and sugar together, add lemon rind. Beat the eggs and add with the flour and fruit. Stir thoroughly together with the milk. Put mixture into a prepared 8½ in (21 cm) cake tin and smooth top. Arrange whole almonds on top of cake. Bake for 3 hr 15 min at 300°F (150°C, Gas Mark 2) or until cooked through.

Preparation: 15 min
Cooking: 1 hr 20 min at
    325°F (170°C, Gas Mark
    3)

10 oz (275 g) self raising
    flour
1 tsp (5 ml) ground ginger
5 oz (125 g) butter
5 oz (125 g) castor sugar
1 tbsp (15 ml) honey
3 eggs
6 fl oz (180 ml) sweet cider

Honey Cream

Preparation: 3 min

4 oz (100 g) icing sugar
4 oz (100 g) butter
1 tbsp (15 ml) honey
4 tsp (20 ml) lemon juice

Cider Cake with Honey Cream

Sift flour with ginger. Cream butter, sugar and honey in mixing bowl. Beat eggs and add with the flour to the creamed mixture. Stir in cider. Pour into a prepared 7 in (18 cm) cake tin. Bake for 1 hr 20 min or until golden brown and cooked through.

Honey Cream
Sift icing sugar, and cream with the butter. Stir in honey and lemon juice, beat well together. Cut cider cake through the middle and use honey cream as a filling, or spread on top of cake as icing.

Preparation: 40 min
Cooking: 1 hr at 325°F
(170°C, Gas Mark 3), and
1 hr at 300°F (150°C, Gas
Mark 2)

1 lemon
1 lb (450 g) apple slices
3 oz (75 g) butter
3 oz (75 g) margarine
8 oz (225 g) soft brown
sugar

10 oz (275 g) self raising
flour
1 tsp (5 ml) nutmeg
1 tsp (5 ml) cinnamon
1 tsp (5 ml) ginger
1 tsp (5 ml) bicarbonate of
soda
4 oz (100 g) dates
4 oz (100 g) currants
4 oz (100 g) sultanas
2 oz (50 g) mixed peel
3 eggs
5 oz (125 g) icing sugar

Lemon Iced Apple Cake

Put apple slices and grated rind of lemon in pan
with 1 tbsp (15 ml) of water. Cook until tender,
then mash into a purée and put aside to cool.
Cream together butter, margarine and sugar. Sift
together flour, spices and soda. Chop dates and
add with the rest of the fruit and flour to the
creamed mixture. Beat eggs, stir into mixture
with apple purée, mix together thoroughly. Pour
into a greased 8½ in (21 cm) cake tin and bake
for 1 hr at 325°F (170°C, Gas Mark 3) and for a
further hour at 300°F (150°C, Gas Mark 2) or
until cooked. Cool on wire rack.

Lemon Icing
Sift icing sugar, mix with 5 tsp (25 ml) lemon
juice. Spoon over top of apple cake.

Preparation: 35 min
Cooking: 20 min at 375°F
(190°C, Gas Mark 5)

5 oz (125 g) self raising flour
5 oz (125 g) castor sugar
5 eggs
1 lb (450 ml) double cream

1 oz (25 g) icing sugar
½ tsp (2.5 ml) vanilla
essence
2 oz (50 g) flaked almonds
raspberry jam
6 glacé cherries
1 piece pink Turkish delight
2 chocolate flake bars

Celebration Gateau

Whisk together castor sugar and eggs in mixing bowl until thick and fluffy. Sprinkle sifted flour on top and gently fold in. Divide mixture between two greased and floured 8½ in (21 cm) sandwich tins. Bake for 20 min. Turn out and cool on rack. Whip cream with icing sugar and essence until thick. Cut sponges through the middle and spread with jam. Spread cream round sides of sponges and roll in flaked almonds, spread cream on sponge tops, place one on top of the other. Put remaining cream in large piping bag with star nozzle. Mark top of sponge into 16 sections with knife, pipe a 'star' or 'bar' in each section, make a large star in the centre. Decorate alternately with glacé cherries, thin slices of Turkish delight and pieces of chocolate flake.

Preparation: 15 min
Cooking: 20 min at 375°F
(190°C, Gas Mark 5)
4 oz (100 g) self raising flour
4 oz (100 g) castor sugar
2 oz (50 g) butter
2 oz (50 g) margarine
2 eggs
1 lemon
5 oz (125 g) icing sugar

Lemon Squares

Put into mixing bowl flour, sugar, butter, margarine, eggs and grated lemon rind. Beat together until smooth. Spread mixture into a prepared swiss roll pan and bake for 20 min. Turn out to cool. Sieve icing sugar and gradually add 5 tsp (25 ml) lemon juice, spread evenly over sponge and cut into squares. (For Orange Squares, make as above, substituting orange for lemon.)

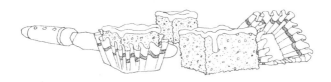

Orange Cake

Preparation: 15 min
Cooking: 15-20 min at 375°F
   (190°C, Gas Mark 5)

1 orange
4 oz (100 g) butter
4 oz (100 g) castor sugar
2 eggs
6 oz (175 g) self raising flour
1 tbsp (15 ml) milk
6 oz (175 g) icing sugar
24 paper cases

Custard Cakes

Preparation: 10 min
Cooking: 20 min at 375°F
   (190°C, Gas Mark 5)

5 oz (125 g) self raising flour
1 oz (25 g) custard powder
pinch of salt, 2 eggs
4 oz (100 g) butter
4 oz (100 g) castor sugar
2 oz (50 g) currants
½ tsp (2.5 ml) vanilla
   essence
1 tbsp (15 ml) milk
24 paper cases

Orange Cakes

Grate orange rind and squeeze juice. Put butter and castor sugar in mixing bowl and cream together with grated rind. Beat eggs and sift flour. Gradually beat eggs into the creamed mixture with a little flour, fold in remaining flour and milk. Arrange paper cases in patty tins and spoon mixture into them. Bake for 15 min or until golden brown. Make orange icing by mixing sifted icing sugar with 6 tsp (30 ml) of strained orange juice. Spoon a little icing on to each cake when they are cool.

Custard Cakes

Sift together flour, custard powder and salt. Cream together butter, sugar and essence. Add beaten eggs with a little of the flour mixture and beat well. Fold in the rest of the flour and the currants, then add milk to make a dropping consistency. Place paper cases in patty tins and distribute mixture evenly between them. Bake for 20 min or until golden and cooked.

Preparation: 45 min
Cooking: 2 hr at 300°F
(150°C, Gas Mark 2), and
1¾ hr at 275°F(140°C,
Gas Mark 1)

5 oz (125 g) plain flour
5 oz (125 g) self raising flour
½ tsp (2.5 ml) grated
nutmeg
1 tsp (5 ml) mixed spice
½ tsp (2.5 ml) salt

6 oz (175 g) currants
8 oz (225 g) sultanas
4 oz (100 g) raisins
2 oz (50 g) cherries
1 orange
8 oz (225 g) butter
8 oz (225 g) castor sugar
4 eggs
1 tbsp (15 ml) milk
Approx 1 lb (450 g) almond
paste
redcurrant jelly

Simnel Cake

Grease and line an 8½ in (21 cm) cake tin. Sift flours, spices and salt together. Pick over clean fruit and chop cherries. Cream butter with sugar and add grated orange rind. Beat in eggs with a little of the spiced flour. Mix fruit and rest of flour, and then fold into creamed mixture with milk. Roll out ⅓ of the almond paste to an 8 in (20 cm) circle. Put ⅔ of the cake mixture into prepared cake tin, cover with almond circle, add remaining cake mixture and smooth top. Bake for 3¾ hr or until cooked through. Turn out to cool on wire rack. Roll out next ⅓ of almond paste to an 8½ in (21 cm) circle. Brush top of cake with a little heated jelly and place almond circle on top. Make remaining almond paste into 11 balls and arrange on top of cake. Brush with beaten egg. Place in a hot oven for 10–15 min or until lightly browned. Alternatively, brown under a hot grill.

Favourite Fruit Cake

Preparation: 20 min
Cooking: 2¼ hr at 350°F
(180°C, Gas Mark 4)

6 oz (175 g) self raising flour
6 oz (175 g) plain flour
8 oz (225 g) margarine
8 oz (225 g) castor sugar
3 oz (75 g) golden syrup
3 large eggs
8 oz (225 g) currants
8 oz (225 g) raisins
4 oz (100 g) mixed peel

Almond Paste

Preparation: 10 min

8 oz (225 g) ground almonds
4 oz (100 g) icing sugar
4 oz (100 g) castor sugar
1 egg
2 tsp (10 ml) lemon juice

Favourite Fruit Cake

Grease an 8 in (20 cm) cake tin and line with greaseproof paper. Sift the two types of flour together, cream margarine with sugar, and beat in the syrup. Gradually add the eggs, beating well. Fold in the sifted flour, fruit and peel, spoon into the prepared tin and smooth the top, then bake in centre of preheated oven. Cool in the tin for 10 min then turn out.

Almond Paste

Place ground almonds in mixing bowl. Sift sugars into bowl and mix together. Beat egg. Add lemon juice to mixture in bowl and as much beaten egg as necessary to make a smooth paste.

Preparation: 35 min
Cooking: 25–30 min at 375°F
 (190°C, Gas Mark 5)
7½ oz (210 g) butter
9 oz (250 g) soft brown
 sugar
3 large eggs

1 tbsp (15 ml) black treacle
6 oz (175 g) self raising flour
1 tbsp (15 ml) cocoa
1 oz (25 g) plain chocolate
1 orange
1 tbsp (15 ml) orange juice
3 oz (75 g) icing sugar

Chocolate Orange Cake

Grease and line two 8 in (20 cm) sandwich tins.
Cream 6 oz (175 g) butter with 6 oz (175 g) soft
brown sugar until mixture is fluffy. Beat in the
treacle and gradually beat in eggs. Sift flour
twice with cocoa, then fold into the creamed
mixture with a metal spoon. Divide the mixture
between the prepared tins and bake in the centre
of preheated oven for 25–30 min or until cooked.
Turn out to cool on rack. Grate and squeeze
orange, melt chocolate, put remaining butter in
pan with the rest of the brown sugar. Heat
gently until melted, add orange rind, juices,
chocolate and icing sugar. Use this to sandwich
cakes together.

Preparation: 20 min
Cooking: 1¾ hr at 400°F
  (200°C, Gas Mark 6)

Pinch of powdered saffron
¼ pint (150 ml) boiling
  water
½ oz (15 ml) fresh yeast

1 lb (450 g) plain flour
pinch of salt
3 oz (75g) butter
3 oz (75 g) lard
2 oz (50 g) castor sugar
4 oz (100 g) currants
4 oz (100 g) sultanas
1 egg

Devonshire Saffron Cake

Mix the saffron with boiling water, then add ¼ pt (150 ml) cold water. Cream the fresh yeast with a little of this liquid then mix in the rest. Sift the flour and salt, rub in butter and lard, stir in sugar and fruit, stir in liquid, mix well. Cover the bowl with a piece of lightly oiled polythene, leave in a warm, not hot, place for 2 hr or until dough is well risen. Grease an 8 in (20 cm) cake tin and line with greased greaseproof paper. Turn risen dough on to a lightly floured surface and knead for 2 min, shape into a round and fit into prepared cake tin, leave in a warm place for 30 min. Brush top of cake with beaten egg, bake in the centre of preheated oven. Turn out to cool and eat that day with butter.

Preparation: 15 min
Cooking: 20 min at 375°F
(190°C, Gas Mark 5)

6 oz (175 g) self raising flour
1 tsp (5 ml) baking powder
3 tsp (15 ml) ground ginger
2 tsp (10 ml) powdered
    cinnamon
2 oz (50 g) butter
2 oz (50 g) castor sugar
1 egg

8 oz (225 g) golden syrup
1 tsp (5 ml) bicarbonate of
    soda
½ teacup boiling water
icing sugar

Butter Icing
Preparation: 10 min
1 oz (25 g) crystallized
    ginger
4 oz (100 g) butter
8 oz (225 g) icing sugar
2 tbsp (30 ml) milk

Ginger Sponge Cake

Brush two 9 in (23 cm) sandwich cake tins with oil, then place a round of greaseproof paper in base of each and brush that with oil. Sift flour, baking powder, ginger and cinnamon into a bowl. Cream butter with sugar until light and fluffy. Beat in the egg with a spoonful of sifted flour. Make a well in the centre of the mixture and pour in the syrup then gradually stir in, followed by the remaining flour mixture. Dissolve the bicarbonate of soda in the boiling water, pour into mixture and stir well. Divide mixture between prepared tins and bake in a moderately hot oven. Allow to cool slightly then turn on to a wire rack to become quite cold before filling. Sandwich the two cakes together with prepared butter icing then dust top of cake with sifted icing sugar.

Butter Icing
Chop crystallized ginger very finely. Cream butter with 2 oz (50 g) of the icing sugar which has been sifted, then add the remaining sifted icing sugar and the milk, beat well. Stir in the chopped ginger. (If preferred this butter icing may be made plain, without the ginger.)

Preparation: 20 min
Cooking: 15–20 min 425°F
(220°C, Gas Mark 7)

1½ lb (675 g) plain flour

½ tsp salt (2.5 ml)
2 oz (50 g) butter
¾ pt (450 ml) milk
1 tsp (5 ml) sugar
2 tsp (10 ml) dried yeast

Devonshire Splits

Sift flour and salt into warmed bowl. Melt butter over gentle heat, leave to cool slightly. Place milk in another saucepan and allow just to warm. Dissolve sugar in this, then sprinkle with dried yeast and leave in a warm place for about 10 min until frothy. Stir into a well in centre of dry ingredients with the melted butter then mix well before turning out on to floured board. Knead well for 5–10 min until quite smooth. Place dough in an oiled polythene bag or put back in the mixing bowl which has been dusted with flour. Cover and leave in a warm place until double in size. Turn on to floured board again and knead lightly. Divide into 16–20 even sized pieces; knead each into a small ball. Set on greased baking tray and press down with hand. Cover and leave to rise until they spring back to the touch. Bake. Cover with a cloth the minute you take them from the oven. When cold, split and spread with strawberry jam and Devonshire cream.

Preparation: 10 min
Cooking: 1¼ hr at 300°F
 (150°C, Gas Mark 2)
1 teacup warm tea

1 teacup mixed dried fruit
1 teacup sugar
2 teacups self raising flour
1 egg

Teabread

Place fruit in mixing bowl with tea and soak overnight. Sift flour and add with sugar to mixture in bowl. Beat egg and stir into the ingredients in bowl. Pour into a prepared loaf tin and bake until cooked. Serve sliced and spread with butter.

Preparation: 20 min
Cooking: 15–20 min at 400°F
   (200°C, Gas Mark 6)
1 lb (450 g) plain flour
2 oz (50 g) lard
2 oz (50 g) currants

1 tsp (5 ml) sugar
5 fl oz (150 ml) milk
5 fl oz (150 ml) water
1 oz (25 g) fresh yeast
2 tsp (10 ml) salt
2 oz (50 g) melted butter

Curranty Cutrounds

Sift flour into mixing bowl. Rub in lard. Stir in currants and sugar. Heat liquids gently until lukewarm. Whisk yeast in half the liquid and dissolve salt in the other half. Add liquids to the flour and mix to a dough. Knead for a few minutes. Place bowl of dough in polythene bag and prove in a warm place. When risen knead lightly on floured surface and roll out to ½ in (1 cm) thick. Cut rounds with a 2½ in (7.5 cm) cutter. Place on greased and floured baking tray. Brush tops with melted butter; prove. Bake at 400°F (200°C, Gas Mark 6) for 15–20 min or until cooked.

Preparation: 20 min
Cooking: 35–40 min at 450°F
    (230°C, Gas Mark 8)
1 lb (450 g) plain flour
½ tsp (2.5 ml) salt

1 oz (25 g) lard
½ oz (15 g) fresh yeast
½ pt (300 ml) tepid milk
2 tbsp (30 ml) clear honey
4 oz (100 g) currants

Fruit Bread

Sift the flour and salt, rub in the lard, cream the fresh yeast with a little of the tepid milk, then stir in the rest. Make a well in the centre of the flour and stir in the yeast liquid and honey to make a soft dough. Turn out on to a lightly floured board and knead for 10 min. Lightly oil the inside of a large polythene bag, put the dough in the bag and leave in a warm, not hot, place for 45 min or until the dough has doubled in bulk. Take dough from bag, knead currants into dough, place into a greased and floured loaf tin 9 in by 5 in (23 cm by 12.5 cm). Leave in a warm place for 15 min. Bake loaf in centre of preheated oven for 35–40 min or until loaf sounds hollow if tapped on the base. Leave to cool. Serve that day with butter. (This bread may be used to make unusual ham sandwiches.)

1 lb (450 g) self raising flour
large pinch of salt
4 oz (100 g) margarine
2 oz (50 g) sugar
4 oz (100 g) currants
9 fl oz (300 ml) milk

Preparation: 15 min
Cooking: 15 min at 450°F
(230°C, Gas Mark 8)

Scones

Sift flour and salt into bowl. Rub in margarine with fingertips to form crumbs. Add sugar and currants, mix together. Stir in milk and make a soft dough. Lightly knead on a floured surface and roll out to ¾ in (2 cm) thick. With a 2½ in (7 cm) cutter cut 22–24 scones, place on a greased baking tray and bake for 15 min or until golden brown.

Cheese, Raisin and Nut Scones
Preparation: 15 min
Cooking: 15 min at 450°F
(230°C, Gas Mark 8)

1 lb (450 g) self raising flour
½ tsp (2.5 ml) baking
powder
pinch of salt
3 oz (75 g) butter
3 oz (75 g) grated cheese
2 oz (50 g) raisins
1 oz (25 g) walnuts
2 eggs
11 fl oz (330 ml) milk

Cherry and Coconut Scones
Preparation: 20 min
Cooking: 15–20 min at 450°F
(230°C, Gas Mark 8)

1 lb (450 g) self raising flour
large pinch of salt
6 oz (175 g) margarine
4 oz (100 g) castor sugar
4 oz (100 g) glacé cherries
2 oz (50 g) coconut
9 fl oz (300 ml) milk

Cherry and Coconut Scones

Cut cherries into quarters. Sift flour and salt into a bowl, and rub in margarine with the fingertips to form crumbs. Mix in sugar, coconut and cherries. Stir in milk, to make a soft dough. Lightly knead on a floured surface and roll out to ¾ in (2 cm) thick. With a 2½ in (6 cm) cutter cut 22–24 scones. Place on a greased baking tray and bake for 15–20 min or until golden brown.

Cheese, Raisin and Nut Scones

Sift the flour, baking powder and salt into a mixing bowl. Rub in the butter with fingertips to form crumbs. Add the cheese, raisins and finely chopped walnuts. Beat eggs and milk, reserve 2 tbsp (30 ml), then add the rest to the mixture to make a soft dough. On floured surface roll out dough to about ¾ in (2 cm) thick, and using a 3 in (7.5 cm) cutter, cut out 18–20 rounds. Brush tops of scones with reserved liquid and place on a greased and floured baking tray Bake for 15 min or until cooked and golden brown.

Peppermint Crisp

Preparation: 12 min
Cooking: 5 min
4 oz (100 g) butter
4 oz (100 g) chocolate
1 tbsp (15 ml) sugar
1 tbsp (15 ml) syrup
1 tbsp (15 ml) cocoa
1 tsp (5 ml) peppermint
    essence
6 oz (175 g) digestive
    biscuits
2 oz (50 g) rich tea biscuits

Preparation: 15 min
Cooking: 5 min
4 oz (100 g) digestive
    biscuits
2 oz (50 g) rich tea biscuits
2 oz (50 g) walnuts
4 oz (100 g) dates
3 oz (75 g) butter
2 oz (50 g) chocolate
2 tbsp (30 ml) syrup
1 tbsp (15 ml) sugar
1 tsp (5 ml) cocoa powder
½ tsp (2.5 ml) vanilla
    essence

Peppermint Crisp

Melt butter, chocolate, sugar, syrup and cocoa together over a gentle heat. Crush biscuits by rolling between layers of greaseproof paper. Add peppermint essence to mixture and then stir in crushed biscuits. Pour into a greased swiss roll pan and smooth surface. Mark into ½ in (1 cm) squares and leave to cool and harden. (To make Chocolate Crisp, omit peppermint essence.)

Date Fingers

Crush biscuits between layers of greaseproof paper with a rolling pin. Chop nuts and cut dates into small pieces. Melt butter, chocolate, syrup and sugar together, then stir in cocoa, essence, walnuts and dates. Lastly add crushed biscuits. Press mixture into a buttered swiss roll pan and mark into fingers. Leave until cold and set, then cut out finger shapes.

Preparation: 15 min
Cooking: 20 min at 350°F
   (180°C, Gas Mark 4)

10 oz (275 g) plain flour
1 tsp (5 ml) grated nutmeg

1 tsp (5 ml) cinnamon
5 oz (125 g) butter
1 oz (25 g) ground almonds
5 oz (125 g) castor sugar
4 oz (100 g) currants
2 eggs

Easter Biscuits

Sift flour and spices into mixing bowl. Rub in butter with fingertips to form crumbs. Stir in almonds, sugar and currants. Beat eggs and add to the mixture to form a firm dough. On a floured surface knead dough and roll out to ⅜ in (1 cm) thick. Using a 4 in (10 cm) cutter, cut 12 rounds. Place on a greased baking tray and bake for 20 min or until brown and cooked. If you prefer a softer biscuit, use self raising flour instead of plain. For a smaller biscuit cut 16 rounds with a 3 in (7.5 cm) cutter.

Preparation: 15 min
Cooking: 20 min at 350°F
  (180°C, Gas Mark 4)
6 oz (175 g) self raising flour
1 oz (25 g) cornflour
pinch of salt
4 oz (100 g) butter
4 oz (100 g) castor sugar
½ tsp (2.5 ml) caraway
  seeds
1 egg
2 tsp (10 ml) milk
½ tsp (2.5 ml) vanilla
  essence

Spicy Biscuits
Preparation: 15 min
Cooking: 15–20 min at 375°F
  (190°C, Gas Mark 5)
4 oz (100 g) self raising flour
pinch of salt
½ tsp (2.5 ml) bicarbonate
  of soda
1 tsp (5 ml) ginger
1 tsp (5 ml) cinnamon
1 tsp (5 ml) mixed spice
2 tsp (10 ml) castor sugar
2 oz (50 g) butter
2 tbsp (30 ml) golden syrup

Seedy Nuts

Sift flours and salt into a mixing bowl, rub in butter with fingertips to form crumbs. Stir in sugar and caraway seeds. Beat egg, milk and vanilla essence together, add to the flour mixture and stir into a firm dough. Take walnut sized pieces, make into balls, flatten with the hand and place apart on a greased and floured baking tray. This mixture makes approximately 24 biscuits. Bake for 20 min or until golden brown.

Spicy Biscuits

Sift together flour, salt, bicarbonate of soda, ginger, cinnamon, mixed spice and sugar. Melt butter and syrup over gentle heat. Allow to cool slightly, then stir into the dry ingredients. Take teaspoon-size pieces and roll into balls, to make about 20. Place balls well apart on greased and floured baking trays. Flatten each slightly and bake for 15–20 min.

Pastry

Preparation: 25 min (plus
    resting time)
8 oz (225 g) plain flour
½ tsp (2.5 ml) salt

3 oz (75 g) butter
3 oz (75 g) lard
¼ pt (150 ml) cold water
1 tsp (5 ml) lemon juice

Flaky Pastry

Sift flour and salt into mixing bowl. Divide fats into four equal parts. Add one part of the fats to the flour and rub in with fingertips to form crumbs. Mix to a soft dough with the liquids. On floured surface knead lightly for 2–3 min. Roll out to a rectangle approximately 15 in.×5 in (37.5 cm×12.5 cm). Dot another part of the fats over the top two-thirds of the pastry. Fold into three and seal edges with the rolling pin. Cover and rest in a cool place for 15 min. Repeat this process twice more, cover and rest pastry in a cool place for 15 min before using. (Makes about 1 lb 2 oz (500 g) of pastry.)

Choux Pastry

Preparation: 15 min
Cooking: 3 min

2½ oz (65 g) plain flour
pinch of salt
¼ pt (150 ml) water
2 oz (50 g) butter
2 medium eggs

Shortcrust Pastry

Preparation: 15 min

8 oz (225 g) self raising flour
pinch of salt
2 oz (50 g) butter
2 oz (50 g) lard
3 tbsp (45 ml) cold water

Choux Pastry

Sift flour and salt into a basin and put in a warm place. Pour water into saucepan and add butter, place on heat and bring to the boil, take off heat immediately it boils. Add warm flour all at once and beat well until mixture leaves sides of pan. Allow to cool slightly. Lightly whisk eggs and add to the cool mixture, beat together thoroughly. Pastry is then ready for use. Add 1 tsp (5 ml) vanilla essence if making for dessert.

Shortcrust Pastry

Sift flour and salt into bowl, rub in butter and lard with fingertips to form crumbs, add water and with a round-bladed knife mix to a dough, knead lightly. The pastry is now ready to use: this recipe makes aproximately 12 oz (325 g).
(Plain flour may be used if liked, but I find self raising flour makes shortcrust pastry lighter and softer for eating.)

Preparation: 10 min
Cooking: 25 min at 400°F
(200°C, Gas Mark 6)
6 oz (175 g) plain flour

pinch of salt
1½ oz (40 g) butter
1½ oz (40 g) lard
2 tbsp (30 ml) cold water

Flan Pastry

Sift flour and salt into a mixing bowl. Rub in butter and lard with fingertips to form crumbs. Mix to a stiff dough with cold water. Roll out to line an 8 in (20 cm) flan dish, then cover pastry with greaseproof paper and baking beans. Bake 'blind' for 15 min, remove greaseproof paper and beans, and bake for a further 10 min, or until cooked. This recipe makes approximately 9 oz (250 gm) pastry.

Preparation: 25 min (plus resting time)

8 oz (225 g) plain flour

½ tsp (2.5 ml) salt
8 oz (225 g) butter
¼ pt (150 ml) cold water
½ tsp (2.5 ml) lemon juice

Puff Pastry

Sift flour and salt into mixing bowl. Rub in quarter of the butter with fingertips to form crumbs. Mix to a soft dough with the liquids. On floured surface knead lightly for 2–3 min. Roll out to a rectangle approximately 15 in×5 in (37.5 cm×12.5 cm). Shape remaining butter to fit inside one half of the pastry rectangle. Fold the other half of the pastry over the top. Seal edges with the rolling pin. Cover and rest in a cool place for 20 min. Roll out to a rectangle 15 in×5 in (37.5 cm×12.5 cm), fold in three and seal edges, cover and rest in a cool place for 15 min. Repeat the second rolling and folding five times, covering and resting pastry for 15 min each time in a cool place. (Makes about 1¼ lb (550 g) of pastry.)

INDEX